50p

THEN AND THERE SERIES
GENERAL EDITOR
MARJORIE REEVES M.A. Ph.D.

Glasgow in the Tramway Age

RONALD W. BRASH M.A.

Illustrated from contemporary sources

LONGMAN

LONGMAN GROUP LIMITED
London

Associated companies, branches and representatives throughout the world

First published 1971

ISBN 0 582 20488 7

Photoset in Malta by St Paul's Press Ltd and Printed in Hong Kong by Dai Nippon Printing Co., (International) Ltd.

FOR DAVID, PETER AND ANNE

ACKNOWLEDGEMENTS

For their assistance in granting research facilities, the author is indebted to the Glasgow City Archivist, Richard F. Dell, B.A. (Oxon), D.A.A., to Mrs Manchester of Baillie's Library, 69 Oakfield Avenue, Glasgow, W.2., and to the staff of the Glasgow Room at the Mitchell Library, Glasgow, and would also like to thank Jack House of the *Glasgow Evening Times*, Henry O. Hellier, N.D.D., A.T.D., of the Glasgow School of Art, Graham E. Langmuir, M.A., L.L.B., and Ian L. Cormack, M.A., for their advice and assistance in the preparation of this book.

For permission to reproduce photographs we are grateful to the following: T & R. Annan, Glasgow, pages 15, 17 *below*, 18 *below*, 28, 35, 42, 47 and 66; Beaverbrook Newspapers, page 7; British Transport Commission, page 27; City Archivist, Glasgow, pages 8, 44 and 54; Miss Greta Lauder Fraser, page 86; Glasgow University, Mackintosh Collection, page 18 *above*; London Transport Board, page 21; Mitchell Library, Glasgow, pages 13, 17 *above left*, 30, 83, 78 and 88; Museum of Transport, Glasgow, pages 11, 55 and 56; Queen's Park Football Club, page 82; Tate Gallery, London, page 22.

Contents

To the Reader 5
1 GLASGOW IN 1914 9
2 TOWN TRANSPORT DURING THE NINETEENTH CENTURY 20
3 THE MEN IN GEORGE SQUARE 35
4 'DALRYMPLE'S CARS' 50
5 A SAIL DOWN THE CLYDE 64
6 THE FESTIVE SEASON 76
HOW DO WE KNOW? 89
THINGS TO DO 92
GLOSSARY 94

To The Reader

On the evening of Tuesday, 4 September 1962, huge crowds were lining the main streets in the centre of Glasgow. They were waiting for a procession to pass by, not of some visiting *celebrities*,* but of something that most of them had known all their lives. For ninety years people had travelled by tram all over Glasgow, but tonight these vehicles would be seen on the city streets for the last time.

Like many cities in the second half of the twentieth century, Glasgow's appearance was changing rapidly, as old buildings were pulled down and replaced by tall concrete office blocks and skyscraper flats. There were plans for new ring roads and motorways that would alter completely the traditional pattern of the streets, and even in the city centre there was to be a system of one-way streets that would change the ways by which people were accustomed to travel. The end of the trams meant the end of an *era* in Glasgow's development which they had done much to create.

In 1760, when Glasgow was the centre for the tobacco trade with the American colonies, it was a small city, centred mainly around the High Street, with a population of about 30,000. By 1820 there were 147,000 people and the city was expanding westwards, taking in a number of surrounding villages. By 1880 there were 704,000 people in Glasgow, and in 1914, just over one million. Although overcrowding near the centre of the city was still a very serious problem, more and more people were living in the *suburbs* as the city spread outwards into the surrounding countryside.

*Words printed in *italics* are explained in the Glossary (p. 94).

In the eighteenth century a rich merchant like the tobacco lord, William Cuninghame, would build his mansion in Queen Street (it still exists as Stirling's Library), within easy walking distance of his place of business at the Cross. A hundred years later wealthy business men would build their large and impressive terrace houses to overlook the Kelvingrove Park, or even as far out as Kelvinside. They might have to travel three or four miles to their offices. At the same time, shopkeepers, skilled tradesmen and office workers were beginning to move into smaller houses and flats away from the bustling city streets, and they, too, would have farther to travel to work. This was taking place in cities all over the world, and was possible because, as you will read in Chapter 2, ways had been found to transport large numbers of people within the towns.

But who was to provide this transport? At first, individuals and private companies did so, but Glasgow was one of the earliest cities to put the transport services in the hands of the Town Council, and run them as a public service. For this reason, the story of the 'Tramway Age' is also the story of the ways in which the city was governed and what this *municipal* government did to make life better for the people it represented. In the period described in this book – that is, between 1890 and 1914 – Glasgow citizens of all sorts seem to have taken a great interest in the way the city's affairs were managed.

Imagine yourself to be standing on the kerb on that September evening in 1962. There is great excitement as the line of trams makes its way down Union Street towards the Argyle Street crossing. A horse tram, drawn by two white horses borrowed specially for this occasion, leads the way, followed by five electric cars, representing the different types of tram seen in the city over the past sixty years. These are to be preserved in a museum to be built in the tramway works. Finally, there are a number of modern trams, carrying members of the public who have managed to get tickets allowing them to travel on them. Some people are putting pennies on the lines so that they will have a souvenir mark as the wheels pass over them. Elderly men have brought their grandchildren to see the cars for the last

The trams run for the last time in Glasgow

time. (Perhaps some of you were there, too, to see a part of local history being made.)

The sky has been overcast for most of the day, although the sun came out for a short time as the procession began its journey. Now, as the last tram disappears over the Jamaica Bridge, it becomes quite dark, and the spectators run for shelter as the rain comes down in torrents.

Buchanan Street in 1914. Traffic is still mainly horse-drawn

1. *Glasgow in 1914*

Now we will change the date and imagine ourselves to be standing at one of the busiest places in the city, the corner of Union Street and Argyle Street, on a warm summer afternoon in 1914. At first many of the buildings seem familiar, but in other respects, the scene is very different from the 1970s. We miss the illuminated signs over shops and restaurants, and stare in amazement at the clothes the people are wearing, especially the ladies with their large hats and long, flowing skirts. The streets are very congested, but the vehicles look strange to us. Most of the vans and lorries are drawn by horses, although we may see an occasional motor vehicle, perhaps a furniture van or a taxicab, passing along the street, taking care not to exceed the twenty miles an hour speed limit. Outside London there are not many motor buses to be found, except in some country districts where they take passengers from outlying villages to the nearest railway station. There are no pedestrian crossings with their flashing orange beacons, and no traffic lights, even at this busy crossing. Instead, a policeman, looking immensely tall in his helmet, and with his dark tunic buttoned up to his neck, stands in the middle of the cross-roads, directing the traffic. At the rush hours, when everyone is going to or from work, he has a very difficult time keeping the long lines of traffic on the move. Yet, unlike modern times, it is not motor cars which cause the traffic block, as in the early 1900s only wealthy people can afford a private car. The most familiar sight would be something no longer seen in our cities – the electric tram.

How many of you have ever travelled on a tram? Probably

not very many, as there are no trams still running anywhere in Great Britain, apart from the line between Blackpool and Fleetwood. They are still quite common in some overseas countries, as you may have seen if you have been abroad. Yet in 1914 trams could be found in almost every large town and city in Britain, and in many smaller places as well. The shining steel grooved rails were laid down the middle of the street, and there were points and crossovers as on a railway. In North America they were given the name of 'street railways'. The cars were driven by electric power, carried in overhead wires. These were suspended above the tracks from thin span wires attached to strong metal poles on each side of the street, or to small diamond-shaped brackets, known as 'rosettes', fixed to the walls of buildings. (Many of these rosettes can still be seen, a sign that there were once tramlines along that particular street.) The tram picked up this electric current through a trolley pole, fixed to its roof, and pressed against the wire by means of a strong spring. You will see that before a tram service could be operated, a great deal of expensive equipment had to be provided, unlike a motor bus which needs no track and carries its own source of power. This is one of the main reasons why, in later years, people decided to replace the trams with buses. Indeed, if the motor bus had been developed by 1900, many of the smaller tramway systems might never have been made.

As in most other places in 1914, Glasgow's trams were double-decked, with a steep curved stair at each end of the car connecting the upper and lower decks. Unlike a bus, a tram has to be able to run in either direction, without being turned round when it reaches its terminus. There is a driver's platform with control handle and brakes at both ends of the car, so that when it reaches the end of the line, the driver moves to the other end, while the conductor pulls the trolley pole off the overhead wire by means of a long rope, swivels it round, and sets it facing in the opposite direction, ready for the return journey. On the lower deck, the passengers sit facing each other on long wooden seats fixed to the sides of the car. On the top deck, there are two rows of double seats facing the direction the car is travelling,

The trams rule the road in Jamaica Street around 1912

with a passage down the middle. The backs of these seats can be pulled over when the car reaches the terminus. (You may have seen an old tram seat being used as a garden bench.)

The early trams were open on top, but this could be very unpleasant in cold or wet weather, so by 1914 most of Glasgow's cars had the tops covered and enclosed with glass windows except for the balconies over the platforms at the top of the stairs. It could be very pleasant sitting out there in good weather. Even today, you will still hear older people on a bus speak of 'going inside' when they are speaking of the lower deck, thus reminding us of the days when the 'outside', or top deck, was open.

We notice that Glasgow trams are kept beautifully painted. The panels below the windows of the bottom deck and round the platforms are painted bright orange. The panels round the top deck display one of five colours: red, blue, green, yellow or white. This is to distinguish the route on which the car runs, and is a very convenient way for passengers waiting at a stop to see whether their car is approaching. Although there are far more than five different tram services, it is usually the case that no two tram routes sharing the same colour will run along the same street. These coloured cars certainly brighten up the drab streets – one writer said they reminded him of Neapolitan ices – and make it easy for you to spot your car at a distance. Regular travellers will speak of taking 'the red car' to Clydebank or 'the blue car' to Govan. At the rush hours, however, when extra cars are needed, you may find a 'blue' car on a 'white' route. Then you have to be careful to look at the destination indicator as well.

If you look at the map and list of routes on pages 61–3 you will see that trams serve almost every part of the city, and that some routes extend beyond the municipal boundary, connecting the city with nearby towns and villages.

The top deck of a tram is an ideal place from which to see the city, so let us make our way to the tram stop in Union Street – a red-painted post labelled ALL CARS STOP HERE in white letters. An elderly man, who is waiting there, sees that we are strangers and offers to help us. He suggests that we should take a 'red' car with ROUKEN GLEN on its destination screen. Rouken Glen, he explains, is a beautiful estate some six miles to the south of the city. Eight years previously it was given to the citizens of Glasgow as a public park through the generosity of a Member of Parliament, A. Cameron Corbett. The tram route was laid down to enable people to visit the park. As he will be going part of the way, he will be able to tell us some of the interesting changes that have taken place in Glasgow within recent years.

We see three trams at the top end of Union Street, and as they
 come towards us, we see that the third one is red. The first, a

yellow car going to Langside, recalls the battle that marked the final defeat of Mary Queen of Scots. The second is a blue car, bound for Renfrew. Its long journey will take it past the busy docks and shipyards that line the south bank of the River Clyde. Our car is not crowded, and we can easily find a seat on the front balcony on top. The car clatters over the tracks which carry the busy east–west routes along Argyle Street, and gathers speed as it approaches the wide Jamaica Bridge over the Clyde. At this point the conductor, dressed in a neat, well-pressed green uniform, comes to collect our fares. It costs twopence to travel the full distance, and our new friend generously offers to pay for us.

He tells us that he has lived in Glasgow for nearly seventy years. 'I was born in Gorbals, the part we are passing through at the moment,' he says. 'Today, we think of the Clyde as running through the centre of Glasgow, but when I was born, Gorbals was not in Glasgow, but was a separate *burgh* on its

The old burgh of Gorbals about 1845

own. There were quite a few of these burghs that have been taken into Glasgow over the years. Pollokshaws, where I live now, only became part of Glasgow two years ago, when the City Boundary was extended to take in two other independent burghs, Govan and Partick, as well as some parts of Lanarkshire, and Renfrewshire, where so many houses had been built that they were really city suburbs in all but name. They could not include Rutherglen in this extension, though. It is an ancient *Royal Burgh*, older than Glasgow and very proud of its independence. The people of Rutherglen feel insulted if anyone calls them Glaswegians!'

We ask him to tell us about other great changes he has seen.

'Well,' he replies, 'it is difficult to know where to begin. The last twenty-five years have probably seen the greatest changes that I can remember. We are now at Eglinton Toll. When the horse trams began running, just over forty years ago, this was the end of the line. A private company owned the cars, and the service wasn't too good. Although they extended the lines a bit further, it wasn't until the Corporation took them over exactly twenty years ago that things really improved. Within five years they had introduced the electric cars that could carry many more people. So more and more families began to move out from the overcrowded parts of the city into the new terrace houses and flats that were being built along the roads near the tram routes. They could travel to their work quickly and in comfort, and it was fairly cheap. As for workers in factories and shipyards – quite a large part of the population – they have special cars laid on for them when they travel to and from their work, and specially reduced fares as well. But you should see the way the trams handle the football crowds. At the international game between England and Scotland a few weeks ago, the Corporation put on two hundred special cars to take the supporters to Hampden Park and to all parts of the city after the game was over. Fifteen years ago, this would have been impossible.'

As he pauses to regain his breath, we ask him if he can recall the most memorable event of those years.

The International Exhibition of 1901 in Kelvingrove Park

'Undoubtedly, it was the International Exhibition of 1901. It was held in the Kelvingrove Park during five glorious summer months. The pavilions made you feel you had been transported to some eastern city, and in them you could see how much science and engineering had progressed over the last half century. There were open air concerts – I particularly enjoyed the American Band under John Philip Sousa, which played so many of his famous marches. At night the whole scene was floodlit. At least we have something to remind us of it in the Art Galleries which were built as the permanent home of Glasgow's many art treasures. You must make sure that you go there some time.'

The car is now nearing Shawlands, and our friend will leave us, soon. There is still so much we want to ask. Does he prefer

Glasgow as it is today or as it was in his younger days?

'I expect you will think that an old *fogey* like me always thinks of the past as better than the present,' he chuckles. 'I don't think there can ever be a better exhibition than the ones I remember in 1888 and 1901, and I must confess that some of these modern dances and ragtime bands that my grandchildren are so keen on don't appeal to me. But at least I can now take them into town and give them an excellent meal in a high-class tearoom, and that is something I could not have done thirty years ago.'

This is very surprising, and we ask the reason why.

'Quite simply, there were no places fit to take ladies or children into for a meal. Businessmen like myself could always have a chop or steak in what we called an 'eating house' but it was no better than a tavern. Drunkenness among young office clerks was unfortunately very common, and caused a lot of concern. Then, a remarkable lady decided that the time had come to open a restaurant where people could enjoy a good meal and a chat with their friends in comfort. Within a few years she had several of these "tea rooms", as she called them, in the centre of Glasgow. This lady's name is Miss Catherine Cranston, and she has set an example not only to Glasgow but to the rest of Britain. But that's not all. She became friendly with a young architect called Charles Rennie Mackintosh. He is a man with very original ideas about how a building should look. He has no time for ornamental pillars and arches, and thinks that we should get back to the plain simple lines of the old Scottish castles and towers. He designed the new College of Art in Renfrew Street, on these lines – rather a shock to those who think it should have been built in the same style as the Art Galleries at Kelvingrove. Anyway, Miss Cranston approves of him. He not only built her latest place, The Willow Tearooms in Sauchiehall Street, but has decorated every room, and designed every piece of furniture and even cutlery for the tables. The only thing he doesn't seem to have done is the cooking!

'Yet, all this improvement really depends on people being able to travel in and around a city of this size. I can't help feeling

Miss Catherine Cranston

Charles Rennie Mackintosh

Glasgow School of Art. Compare this with the Kelvingrove Art Galleries shown on page 42 which look much older but were built about the same time

A room in Miss Cranston's Willow Tearooms

The waterfalls in Rouken Glen Park

that this is where Glasgow has scored over other places. If you want proof of that, ask anyone whom they consider to be the best-known man in the corporation. I'm prepared to guess that for every one person that can tell you the name of the Lord Provost, there are ten who know the Tramway Manager, Mr James Dalrymple. He has tremendous faith in the trams and what they can still do to develop the city, and his favourite saying is "We've still a long way to go." Some people think he will go too far and land the city with more than it can afford, but no one can deny that he knows his job and loves it. The tramways may be owned by the city, but most people think of them as "Dalrymple's cars".'

The tram is now threading its way through the narrow streets of Pollokshaws, the tracks taking up almost the entire width of the road. As it climbs a steep hill towards a church and a group of large grey stone *villas*, we can see the open fields and moorlands of Renfrewshire just beyond them. We have reached the end of the built-up area, and here our good friend has to bid us farewell. We think of all the interesting facts on Glasgow's development he has told us about, as the car takes us out into the country and through the small village of Thornliebank before stopping at the gates of Rouken Glen. Perhaps in future years there will be an unbroken line of houses between here and the city, and Thornliebank, like many another isolated village, will find itself growing into another suburb. The coming of the tramways has certainly made it possible.

2 *Town Transport during the Nineteenth Century*

We have seen that, as towns grew larger, the need for some means of taking people to and from their work became more urgent. The stage coaches were a familiar sight in the 1820s before the railways arrived to put them out of business. They carried passengers between towns, and into the nearest town from the outlying villages, often setting them down at the door of some coaching inn. Your fare depended on the distance you had travelled, as on a modern bus, and it cost more to ride inside the coach than it did to travel outside with the driver and the guard. However, the number of people a stage coach could hold was small – usually not more than a dozen – and a larger vehicle, running within the city and picking up its passengers as they wished, would be a great benefit to people who wanted to travel within the town itself.

As we might expect, it was in London that this new type of public coach first appeared. On 4 July 1829 George Shillibeer began a service of coaches between Paddington and the Bank. They were called 'omnibus', from a Latin word meaning 'for everyone', and soon became known as 'buses' for short. The first buses were long, having three windows along each side. They could seat twenty passengers, who sat, ten on each side, on long benches facing each other. They seem to have been popular from the start as Charles Dickens tells us in 'Sketches by Boz', one of his earliest works: 'Of all the public *conveyances* that have been constructed since the days of the Ark – we think that is the earliest on record – to the present time, commend us to an omnibus.'

 No one was allowed to travel by omnibus unless he could find a

George Shillibeer's Omnibus, 1829

seat, but it seems that even this difficulty could be got round, if it meant that the conductor could collect an extra fare. Again Charles Dickens tells us:

> We are not aware that it has ever been precisely *ascertained* how many passengers our omnibus will contain. The impression on the cad's [conductor's] mind evidently is, that it is amply sufficient for the accommodation of any number of persons that can be enticed into it. 'Any room?' cries a very hot pedestrian. 'Plenty o' room, sir,' replies the conductor, gradually opening the door, and not disclosing the real state of the case, until the wretched man is on the steps. 'Where?' inquires the entrapped individual, with an attempt to back out again. 'Either side, sir,' rejoins the cad, shoving him in, and slamming the door. 'All right, Bill.' Retreat is impossible; the new-comer rolls about, till he falls down somewhere, and there he stops.

Why was the conductor so keen to cram as many people on his

Inside a London omnibus 1850

bus as he possibly could? We cannot imagine a bus conductor today wanting to make his job of collecting fares more difficult than it is. But we must remember that George Shillibeer did not long remain as the only operator of omnibuses. Other men saw how they could make money out of carrying people from one part of London to another, and fierce competition began between rival bus owners for customers. Here is another incident, describing how a 'pirate bus' seized a passenger as he was about to board another vehicle:

A second omnibus comes up and stops immediately behind us. Another old gentleman elevates his cane in the air, and runs with all his might towards our omnibus . . . the door is opened to receive him, he suddenly disappears – he has been spirited away by the opposition. Hereupon the driver of the opposition taunts our people with his having 'regularly done them out of that old swell', and the voice of the 'old swell' is heard vainly protesting against this unlawful detention. We rattle off, the other omnibus rattles after us, and every time we stop to pick up a passenger, they stop to take him up too; sometimes we get him, sometimes they get him; but whoever don't get him say they ought to have had him, and the cads of the respective vehicles abuse one another accordingly.

The next step was to make more room for extra passengers by fixing a ladder at the back end of the bus and inviting the more active gentlemen passengers to travel 'outside' on the roof. They sat back-to-back on two long benches fixed to the centre of the roof – this was known as a 'knifeboard' – and rested their feet on a board attached to each side of the roof above the windows. It cannot have been very comfortable, especially on wet or windy days. Yet side panels were not put round the top deck to protect the legs from the wind and rain until years later, and it was later still before covered tops on buses were allowed, as people thought they would make the bus top-heavy. Our Victorian traveller was not frightened of getting wet when he travelled by bus.

The horse bus became more popular than ever by 1845, when it could be found not only in London but also in a number of provincial towns as well. In Glasgow, there was fierce rivalry between two omnibus proprietors, Duncan MacGregor and Andrew Menzies (pronounced Ming-es). They looked – and acted – more like characters in a Western film than city businessmen, but they did make it possible for Glasgow people to travel all over the city swiftly and cheaply. Twopence was the highest fare charged. To make the competition more exciting, Menzies and MacGregor, who were both Highlanders, painted their buses in their own tartans, and the travellers supported their favourite buses as we might support our favourite

Andrew Menzies

football team. This rivalry lasted for over twenty years. By then, Andrew Menzies owned no less than fifty buses and five hundred horses to pull them.

There was another side to the story, however. Listen to this report of traffic conditions in the streets of London, which appeared in 'The Times' on 3 December 1858:

> At any hour between ten and five, you are sure to find some part of our main thoroughfares a solid pack of vehicles, unable to move one way or the other, and full of unfortunates who would give anything to reach their destinations . . . They look at their watches, they crane out of the windows of cab or bus, they mutter savagely. All is in vain . . . before them is an endless train of omnibuses, light carts, heavy vans, brewer's waggons, *hansoms*, four wheeler trucks, some turned this way, some turned that, all *indissolubly* locked. At length there is a slight movement. The ice-field shifts. They advance a few yards and then another *deadlock*.

Take away the hansom cabs and this might quite easily be a description of a main street in any of our cities today. How did they propose to get over this terrible problem of congestion?

An American business man, George Francis Train, happened to be visiting England at this time. Starting his career in the family shipping office in Boston, Massachusetts, he had already travelled all over the world, and at the age of thirty was a wealthy man. If you have read Jules Verne's novel, 'Around the World in Eighty Days', you may like to know that the adventures of Phileas Fogg were based on Train's experiences. Train was always interested in any new forms of travel, and in America he had been most impressed by the 'street railways' he had seen in Philadelphia. There, he had seen coaches, fitted with *flanged* wheels to run on rails laid in the main streets, being pulled by two horses (the same number as were used to haul a bus) but able to carry no less than sixty passengers. This, he was sure, was the answer to London's traffic problems, and he wrote a pamphlet entitled 'Observations on street railways' in support of it:

> Each railway car displaces two omnibuses and four horses, thus relieving the street of one of the main causes of the oft-recurring lock-ups. The wear and tear from these omnibuses being transferred to the rail, the ratepayers save a

> large percentage in taxes. The cars move faster than the omnibuses and so gentle is the motion, the passenger can read his journal [newspaper] without difficulty.

As it happened, the honour of having the first street railway – or 'tramway' as it was called in Britain – was held not by London but by the Merseyside town, Birkenhead. Train formed a private company to run the cars, after the Commissioners had given him permission to lay down $1\frac{1}{4}$ miles of track from Woodside Ferry to Birkenhead Park. On 30 August 1860 passengers were able to ride on a tram for the first time in Britain when this short line was opened. There were four cars, two double-deck and two single-deck, and the passengers seem to have liked them very much, according to one report from the 'Illustrated London News'. 'Travelling by one of Mr Train's carriages, as contrasted with one of our ordinary omnibuses, is like quitting a narrow and confined room for a *commodious* and well-ventilated apartment.'

He was not so fortunate when he opened three tram routes in London. People objected to the rails in the streets, and the London General Omnibus Company, who regarded the trams as their rivals, claimed that in one day three accidents to other road vehicles had occurred, all because of the tram tracks. Finally, the Sheriff of Surrey ordered men to start lifting the tracks while the cars were still running. Train gave up the idea of building any more tramways in Britain, and returned, in disgust, to the United States.

His work was by no means in vain. The Birkenhead tramways continued, and other lines were built in some northern towns where they proved to be more popular than in the south. He will be remembered particularly for introducing three things that we take for granted on our buses today but were never seen before his time: uniforms for the driver and conductor, warning bells to let the driver know when all passengers were on board, and permission for people to stand on the lower deck when all seats were taken, with leather straps for them to hold on to. On the next cold, wet day when we are allowed to

The first tram in London, 1860

stand in a crowded bus instead of being told to wait for one with vacant seats, let us remember this remarkable American, George Francis Train.

Ten years later, in 1870, Parliament decided that, as more and more towns wanted to run tramways, special *legislation* would be needed to see that the rights that every person enjoyed on the public highways would be looked after, and that the cost of keeping the roads in good repair would be partly met by the people who ran the cars. It therefore passed the Tramway Act for this purpose. Many of its clauses are rather difficult to understand for those of us who are not lawyers or transport officials, but three points are very important to our story, and can be summed up in these words:

1. Town Councils had the right to say whether or not they were willing to have tramways in their towns.
2. Town Councils could own the car lines but were not allowed to run trams on them. This was to be done by private companies but the Councils could take them over after they had been running for twenty-one years.
3. The roadway between the car lines and for eighteen inches on either side of it had to be maintained by the owners of the car lines.

This explains why cobbled stones were laid between car lines and on each side of them, even when the rest of the roadway was covered with a surface of tar or *asphalt*. When track had to be relaid, it was cheaper to lift and replace cobbles than to break up a road surface.

From this time most British cities and large towns had tramways in their main streets. Glasgow was one of these. The Town Council laid a 2½-mile route from St George's Cross along the New City Road, Cambridge Street Sauchiehall Street, Renfield Street and the Jamaica Bridge to Eglinton Toll in 1872. By the Tramway Act, they could not operate the cars but had to allow a private company to do so on a twenty-two years *lease*. On the afternoon of 19th August, the opening ceremony took place:

> The Lord Provost, Magistrates, and Town Council, and a large number of gentlemen assembled at St George's Cross in order to formally open the line. Seven cars were brought from the depot in Cambridge Street and ranged along the

Glasgow's Jamaica Bridge in the 1880s, showing the original privately-owned horse cars

Great Western Road – two or three being drawn by three horses abreast and one in front with *postillions* in uniform, while the others were drawn by two horses abreast and one in front with postillion. The crowd assembled to witness the ceremony was very large.

It was a good beginning for the Glasgow Tramway and Omnibus Company, and for its manager, our old friend Andrew Menzies. Unfortunately he died in the following year, and it was a solicitor named John Duncan who took charge of the company. Within a few years the tram lines had been extended to many parts of the city. North of the river they went as far as Whiteinch, Kelvinside, Maryhill and Springburn. On the south side they reached Mount Florida, Pollokshaws, and the Govan boundary at Paisley Road Toll. In 1893, the Company carried 54 million passengers in one year and owned 300 trams and over 3,000 horses.

But the Company's days were numbered. The lease would end in 1894, when the Town Council could take over and run the tram services if they wished to do so. About this time the city boundary was extended. Not only districts in the surrounding counties of Lanark, Renfrew and Dunbarton, but also six independent small burghs – Hillhead and Maryhill in the north, Govanhill, Crosshill, Pollokshields, and Pollokshields East, in the south – all became part of Glasgow. (You can see where they are on the map inside the front cover.) Glasgow Town Council already supplied these places with water and gas. Why should the tramways not likewise be a municipal service?

At the next election of the Town Council, the Glasgow citizens were asked if they wanted the Council to take over the tramways, and a majority supported this idea. Many people complained that the company was not giving as good a service as it should. The cars were cramped and dirty. The fares were too dear. The drivers and conductors were paid low wages yet had to work long hours – sometimes as much as fifteen hours a day. This was bad for their health, and dangerous for the

'Can you find me a seat.' The stout lady's predicament shows how cramped were the horse trams owned by the private Company

passengers. When the Council tried to make the Company improve working conditions, John Duncan retorted that he could not afford to raise wages or shorten working hours without raising fares. It was a deadlock. When the Council said they would take over the service in 1894, the Company refused to sell any of the cars, horses or *depots*. They thought the Council would not be able to carry out their plan, and would have to ask them to continue after all.

The Council decided to go ahead, in spite of this. It was a race against time as within two years they must be ready to run a full tram service on the day after the Company gave it up. Apart from the tracks, which they owned already, they would have to start from scratch. Let us see what would have to be done:

1. Nine new depots and stables attached to them had to be built.
2. 300 new cars, better than the company's cars, had to be bought.
3. Over 3,000 horses, suitable for this work, had to be found, and they and their drivers trained for the work.
4. Arrangements had to be made for making harness, shoeing of horses, obtaining *provender* and straw bedding and for grooming and *veterinary* care of the horses.
5. More than 2,000 men had to be engaged, and trained, as drivers and conductors. In addition, they would need blacksmiths, saddlers, grooms, depot foremen, and veterinary surgeons, as well as clerks and cashiers to work in the tramway office.
6. Above all, they would need a good Tramway Manager.

Neither John Duncan nor any of his assistants was willing to work for the Council. Fortunately, the right man was available. He already worked for the Council as head of the Cleansing Department. His name was John Young. He was born and brought up on a farm near Bishopton in Renfrewshire and had been *dux* at Paisley Grammar School, but instead of going on to the university, where he would have done well, he preferred to return to the farm, and later take up employment in Glasgow. He had a great love of horses and knew a great deal about them.

John Young

Also he could tackle difficulties without getting flustered. Finally, he could work with other people and get the best out of them.

At midnight on Saturday, 30 June 1894, the last Company car trundled into the depot, and its horses were unharnessed for the last time. Next morning, as the sun shone brightly on the people going to church, the streets echoed to the sounds of horses' hooves as they drew the brand new cars painted dark maroon on the lower deck. Around the open top decks, in place of the advertisements the former cars had carried, the panels were painted in one of the five route colours mentioned in chapter 1, which were to become in the *hallmark* of the trams from that time. The drivers and conductors wore well-cut uniforms of dark green *serge* and had brass cap badges. They were to work a ten hour day and be paid 24 shillings per week (The

Company had paid their men 21 shillings per week for working at least twelve hours a day). When the people crowded on to the new cars, they had another surprise – a new halfpenny fare for short journeys. The cars were roomier and much cleaner. Moreover they really belonged to the citizens of Glasgow.

John Young must have been relieved to see his cars ready on time. Only three weeks earlier, over half the new horses had taken ill with influenza. Most of them recovered, but it showed

Passengers enjoy a trip on a new Corporation tram

how hazardous a job it could be, especially as the Company still had a number of horse buses which, they hoped, would deprive the new trams of passengers and make the new business a costly failure. Within a few weeks it was the other way round. As we shall see in a later chapter, the municipal tramways made greater profits than anyone had ever imagined.

It had other far-reaching results. From this time, interest in the affairs of the city began to increase among all classes of people. John Young's successor, James Dalrymple, put the matter in a nutshell some years later when speaking to an American visitor to the city. We shall meet both of these gentlemen later on in this book.

> The opening of the trams in 1894 coincided with, many people would say it was the cause of, the rebirth of *civic* enthusiasm that has characterised the last ten years of the life of the city. Undoubtedly, the more things the city does for the people, the more the people are interested in the city.

About this time, the Town Council was given the official title of 'The Corporation of Glasgow'. We shall therefore refer to it as the 'Corporation'. To find out more about it, we shall need to make our way to George Square and the large building on its east side, the City Chambers. Here we shall meet the members of the Corporation, and find out something of the work they have to do.

3 The Men in George Square

The City Chambers is the largest and most important of Glasgow's municipal buildings. It is the place where the Corporation meets to discuss the city's affairs. It is here that distinguished visitors to the city are met and entertained by the Lord Provost. A number of important officials like the Town Clerk and the City Chamberlain have their offices in the building. Finally it has special rooms where any citizen who has any problem or complaint can have a talk with one of his local councillors and ask for his help or advice.

George Square and the City Chambers

What do we mean by a councillor? How does he get elected to the Corporation? The city is divided into a number of districts, known as wards. Each ward is represented by three councillors. Each year a municipal election is held when one of these councillors must retire, but can be re-elected if he so wishes and if sufficient people in the ward want him to continue to represent them. Normally a councillor is appointed for three years, but should he want to retire from the council because of ill-health or for any other reason before his time is up, a special election can be held in that ward to find someone to take his place. Sometimes at the annual election no one wants to oppose the standing councillor. In that case, no election is held, and that ward is said to be 'uncontested'.

Now that we know who the councillors are, let us see how they set to work governing this large city, during our period. Fortunately, we have a very full and interesting account of their work by an American professor named Frederic Clemson Howe, who paid a visit to Glasgow in 1905. He was gathering material for an important book he was writing on European cities, and he made a point of talking to as many people as possible from all walks of life. He begins by describing Glasgow as 'in many ways the most aggressively efficient city in Great Britain', and goes on to tell us of his first meeting with a group of councillors at a city business club:

> I was introduced to a knot of sandy-haired business men. They were deep in talk. I heard of tramways, of gas, of electricity and of telephones. And especially of some big Corporation in which they all seemed to be interested. One of the men was a shipowner, another a large merchant, another an editor – all were men of *eminence*.

Not every councillor belonged to a group such as this, of course. Nor would many of them be as well-off as these men seemed to be. Yet it was not easy for working men to find the time to attend Corporation meetings, which took place on alternate Thursday afternoons, and not suffer a loss in income.

 If a councillor were a miner or an engine driver, he might have to work on the night shift for many years. Councillors, then as now, were not paid for this work, and it is not surprising that it took a man of determination to take up this work.

Mr Howe then went to meet the Lord Provost, Sir John Ure Primrose. He was in the flour milling business and had been a member of the Corporation for twenty years. Although he had been appointed to the highest post in the Corporation by the other members in 1902, he was still an elected representative for his ward, just as the Prime Minister is a Member of Parliament representing a *constituency*. Mr Howe gives us a glimpse of how Sir John's day might be spent:

> He is the busiest man in the city. At the Town Hall by ten, the morning is filled with correspondence and the sessions of committees. Then an official luncheon. Later, perhaps a meeting of the council, over which he presides, with frequent interruptions to attend some public gathering. In the evening a dinner, a congress or fair to be opened with a speech. Later, another address, possibly before some working men's organisation.

He would not seem to have much time left to spend at home with his family and friends. It is, however, a very great honour to be the First Citizen and to act as host to the many famous people who come to Glasgow on official visits. He is usually knighted by the monarch during his term of office. He has an official conveyance to take him about the city. In 1905 it was a coach drawn by two horses. Today he has a saloon car. It is easily recognised as it carries the unusual numberplate G O.

To understand how the Corporation organises its work, we shall have to consider the first meeting to be held after the annual election which took place in the previous November. Let us imagine ourselves to be sitting in the public gallery of the Council Chamber, where the meetings take place. The seats where the coucillors sit are arranged in *tiers* to form a semicircle facing the Lord Provost's chair and those of the Senior Magistrate and the Town Clerk. There are also seats at the side for any corporation officials who may be asked to be present at a council meeting. The Chief Constable, the City Surveyor, or the Medical Officer of Health are some of these people who frequently have to attend such meetings to give the councillors expert advice.

Promptly at 2.15 p.m. the councillors stand up as the Lord Provost, preceded by the Town Officer carrying the *mace*, enters the chamber from the Provost's Room and takes his seat. The Corporation is now said to be 'in session'.

A meeting of Glasgow Corporation in 1910

If every member is present, there should be seventy-seven councillors at this meeting. There are twenty-five wards now in Glasgow, and each has roughly the same number of people living in it. This means that there are more wards in the central parts of the city where more people live, than in the suburban districts where the houses are not built so closely together. From time to time, the ward boundaries may be changed as new houses are built away from the city centre.

 Perhaps you have noticed that there are two more councillors than we might expect – seventy-seven instead of seventy-five. This is because two of them do not represent wards but are elected by the Merchants' House and the Trades' House respectively as the Dean of Guild and the Deacon Convener. They remind us of the days when the merchants and craftsmen of the city formed a 'closed corporation', and no one else could have any say in the running of the city. (You can read all about this in another book in this series, entitled 'Glasgow and the Tobacco Lords'.) They still have a very important part to play in the city's affairs. No new streets or buildings can be made or existing ones altered or extended without the Dean of Guild's permission. In this way, the Corporation has some control over the way the city develops.

As this is the first meeting after the election, a number of posts have to be filled. The Lord Provost normally serves for three years, so Sir John Ure Primrose will not retire for another year. However, there may be some vacancies among the fourteen magistrates who are known as Bailies, and these will be filled by choosing a number of councillors for this important work. They assist the Lord Provost in entertaining important visitors, and the Senior Bailie will always act as chairman of a meeting of the Corporation if the Provost cannot be there. Their main duty is to preside at the local police courts where anyone charged with committing a minor offence may be fined or sent to prison for a short period, if found guilty. However, if the Bailie thinks that the crime deserves a more severe sentence than he is allowed to give, he will *remit* the accused person to the Sheriff Court. The Sheriff, unlike the Bailie, is always a fully qualified lawyer. The Bailie is always guided in legal matters by a lawyer from the Town Clerk's Office, but is free to give advice or warning to those people brought before him, to keep out of further trouble or they will be dealt with more severely the next time they appear in court.

A councillor must now be appointed as City Treasurer. Next to the Lord Provost he has the hardest job of any Corporation member as it is his duty to see how much money will be required for the coming year for the many public services run by the Corporation, and whether the city can afford to extend or improve them. He has to decide how the money is to be raised. Some of it comes from what people have to pay for using them, like gas and electricity bills and tram fares. Some of it is lent by *investors* and the Corporation has to pay them interest on this money. But most of the money comes from the *rates* which have to be paid each year to the City Chamberlain by every householder and every person or company owning offices, shops, factories, or any other property within the city boundary. Of course the Treasurer does not have to do all this work unaided. The City Chamberlain and his staff are highly qualified in financial matters and it is their job to see that rates are paid, money supplied to the various departments for wages and other expenses, and accounts properly kept. Yet it is the Treasurer who has to explain and justify what the Corporation spends each year, not only to the other councillors but also to the ratepayers.

It did not take Mr Howe very long to find out how great an interest in civic affairs was taken by a large number of the citizens, both rich and poor. He had been talking to a man on the top deck of a tramcar about the rates and how they were used to provide services for the people of Glasgow, when his companion pointed to a group of working men enjoying a game of bowls in a public park: 'Any one of these men could tell you the things I am telling you. They regard the trams, the gas, the electricity, the water as their business. A council man has got to attend to the business of these men. If they don't, they *heckle* the life out of him.' It is not surprising to find Mr Howe coming to the conclusion that 'the fear of the ratepayer is present in every councilman's breast'.

We have used the words 'public services' several times. We shall understand what this means if we listen carefully to the next business of the Council, which is the appointment of the various committees. It would be impossible for the full council to make decisions on the running of every department, and so each has its own committee of between twenty to thirty councillors who take a special interest in its affairs. One of them is made chairman or convener of that committee and acts as the Lord Provost does at Council meetings. Every councillor can expect to be asked to serve on at least six committees and perhaps act as convener of one or two of them. The Lord Provost is automatically a member of each committee, although he will not have the time to attend every meeting.

In 1904 twenty-one Standing Committees were set up. These show us how widespread was the Corporation's work by that time.

1. Finance (the City Treasurer is always convener of this committee)
2. Public halls
3. Churches and churchyards (that is, those owned by the corporation)
4. Parliamentary Bills
5. Municipal buildings
6. Libraries
7. Police, street lighting and Fire Brigade
8. Roads
9. Cleansing and refuse collection
10. Public baths and washhouses
11. Sewage disposal
12. Building regulations
13. Parks and open spaces
14. Tramways
15. Markets and slaughterhouses
16. Gas
17. Electricity
18. City improvements (mainly concerned with slum clearance)
19. Water
20. Health (hospitals, clinics and prevention of disease)
21. Telephone (Glasgow ran its own telephone service from 1900 to 1907.

When we realise that each of these committees represents a Corporation department and that in each department there will be a manager, his staff, and perhaps several thousand employees, we can see how big a part these 'public services' play in the lives of every city dweller. It is good to remember also the amount of 'spare time' that a councillor would need to give to Council matters.

After the committees have been appointed, the first Council meeting is over. At later meetings they will hear and consider reports from these various committees. Sometimes, however, a tour of inspection takes place so that they can see for themselves how the work is progressing.

Mr Howe took part in one of these tours, and he has given us this account of it:

> We drove to the municipal lodging house designed to afford a home for widows and widowers with children. It is provided with *kindergartens* and *crèches* in which the young children are left when the parent goes out to work. We visited the slum clearance enterprise and municipal dwellings erected on the site of one of the most disease-breeding spots in Britain. We visited the central fire-department station and saw the firemen at work in the shops building and repairing fire engines, wagons and equipment. We

A public bowling green. Kelvingrove Art Galleries are in the background

passed numerous bowling greens as smooth as billiard tables, where working men spend the long summer evenings at the favourite Scotch play of bowls. The inspection closed with a banquet at the city hall at which the chairmen of the various committees discussed the achievements of the past year and their hopes for the future.

He also tells us that these civic-minded working men 'knew how much was spent on wines and luncheons, and there was some protest against the wine bill which is one of the little extravagances that arouse much talk at elections and in the *radical* press'. Perhaps we might agree that after all these long meetings they deserved an occasional treat!

It is also worth remembering that in 1905 there were many people who could clearly remember the days when almost none of these good things existed. In 1840 the city's water supply was drawn either from the River Clyde or from a number of wells, many of which were so badly *contaminated* that thousands died in the epidemics of typhus and cholera that ravaged the city from time to time. Yet by 1859 the Corporation had built a great *aqueduct* thirty miles long to bring plentiful supplies of fresh water from Loch Katrine in the heart of the Trossachs, at the foot of Ben Lomond. Along with a smaller *reservoir* in the moors of Renfrewshire – known as the Gorbals Waterworks – this water supply not only ensured that Glasgow and the places around it would never go short, but it cut the rate of disease drastically. In a cholera outbreak in 1866 sixty-six people died; in a similar outbreak in 1854, nearly four thousand people had been wiped out.

Fresh water, however, was not enough to stop disease from spreading. As the city grew, the problem of disposing of *sewage* became worse. One of the reasons why towns often grew up on the banks of a river was that the river could serve as a drain, and Glasgow was no exception. By the last quarter of the nineteenth century, the Clyde, particularly at low tide in hot weather, had become so smelly that one writer even called it 'The Sewage Canal'.

Lord Provost Sir John Ure Primrose, wearing his chain of office, and the councillors at the Annual Inspection of the waterworks

> The volume of filth thrown into it renders the river little better than an open sewer, the contents of which exhale an evil odour perceived a long way from its banks, and which, churned up by propellors and paddles of steam vessels, yield in summer an almost intolerable stench. Truly the price we pay for our highly organised condition of city life is very heavy!

In 1891 the Corporation began to build a large sewage works at Dalmarnock, on the boundary of Glasgow and Rutherglen. A few years later, a similar system was opened at Dalmuir to the west of the city. The energetic Mr Howe tells us of his visit to it in 1905:

> I went to the sewage disposal works at Dalmuir. An old employee took me in tow. He explained how the sewage was collected, how it was separated by chemical treatment, how the water was purified before being poured into the

River Clyde. It was so pure, he said, that it was fit to drink. He offered me a glassful but I told him I was not feeling thirsty just at that moment. So he drank it himself.

The superintendent of the Dalmarnock works used to say that he used the purified water for his goldfish bowl. As well as making the Clyde much fresher and healthier, the city made money by selling the solid material as fertiliser or using it on the farms they owned on the outskirts of the city. What could not be used – the *sludge* – was taken in special steamers and dumped in a deep part of the Firth of Clyde off the island of Bute. The Corporation thus became shipowners as well, the ships being called, appropriately, 'DALMARNOCK', 'DALMUIR' and 'SHIELDHALL' (after a third works opened in 1910 to deal with the south side of the river).

The sludge disposal steamer, 'Dalmuir'

Health played a very big part in the Corporation's work in other ways too. Public parks were opened in all parts of the city so that men, women and children, cooped up in over-crowded *tenement* buildings, could enjoy fresh air and exercise.

Rouken Glen, as we saw in Chapter 1, was given to the city by a generous landowner. He also gave up a large piece of mountainous country near Lochgoilhead in Argyllshire, and many people could enjoy a day's sail by river steamer, and a chance – perhaps their only chance – to explore mountain paths and inhale good hill air, while remaining on land owned by Glasgow Corporation.

Ardgoil Estate. A Glasgow Corporation Park in the mountains of Argyllshire near Lochgoilhead

At the same time, we must not forget that, with all these changes, Glasgow was a desperately overcrowded city with some of the worst housing in Europe. A Royal Commission, set up in 1912 to look into the problem of overcrowding, found that in Scotland generally, the number of times a family was to be found living in one room (known as a 'single-end'), or in two rooms (the 'but-and-ben') was six times greater in proportion to the population than was to be found in England and Wales. Moreover, as Scottish cities normally built great blocks of houses, five or six storeys high and divided into flats, the

A back court in the Saltmarket, 1868

people who lived in these tenements were literally very much on top of one another, and often had to share too few water taps and lavatories.

Here is a report, published in 1888, by a medical officer of health, on the results of overcrowding:

> Of all the children who die in Glasgow before they complete their fifth year, 32 per cent die in houses of one apartment; and not 2 per cent in houses of five apartments and upwards. There they die, and their little bodies are laid on

a table or on the dresser, so as to be somewhat out of the way of their brothers and sisters who play and sleep and eat in their ghastly company. One in every five of all who are born there never see the end of their first year.

This is a horrifying story, and examples of it could be found in many industrial towns at this time, where people were housed in such vile conditions. Although it was not till 1919 that *council houses* began to be built to relieve this overcrowding, Glasgow began to tackle this problem many years before that, as part of a campaign against slums, squalor and poor health, especially among children.

In 1866, by Act of Parliament, the City Improvements Trust was set up. This came, in time, under the Corporation with its own committee. It began by buying up land around Glasgow Cross, demolishing scores of old houses and laying out new wide streets with proper lighting, paving and drains. At first it was hoped that private landowners would build good modern tenements to let to families, but as many people lost their money when the City of Glasgow Bank failed in 1878 the Corporation decided, some years later, to build blocks of houses and let the flats in them to families not able to afford the rents charged for better types of privately rented houses. After 1897, when they were allowed to do this, modern and well built blocks of tenements were put up, and remain today, in parts of Old Glasgow like the Saltmarket, and in areas farther away, where farming land was purchased specially for this purpose. These houses were well furnished with large windows to let in light, water in each flat, good fireplaces and gas lighting. For unmarried men and women there were hostels known as 'Model Lodging Houses', where, at a cost of sixpence a night, the lodger had a comfortable bed in its own small room, could wash his clothes, cook his food and eat it in a dining hall, and even buy food in a special shop in the building. Finally, as Mr Howe told us, there was a special centre where widows and widowers could have their children looked after while they were at work, and so could keep their families together. Glasgow certainly did not solve the problem of how to end slums, but the Corporation can take the credit of doing so much to show how a start might be made.

At the end of his visit, Frederic Howe summed up his impressions of Glasgow, as he saw it, in these words:

> Enthusiasm, and interest, devotion and pride – these are the characteristics of Glasgow citizenship. I have talked with the heads of city departments, with a score of town councillors, with police and fire officials, with clerks, bathhouse custodians, and conductors on tramcars, with all sorts of men, from the Lord Provost down to the cab driver. And this is the only citizenship I have been able to find.

He had one final call to make. Of all the Corporation departments, it was the tramways and the men in charge of them that were most frequently praised. He could not leave Glasgow without meeting Mr Dalrymple.

Kennyhill flats, built by the Glasgow Improvements Trust in 1910

4 *'Dalrymple's Cars'*

Let us now accompany Frederic Howe as he leaves the City Chambers and makes his way along St Vincent Street and up the hilly Renfield Street. He may have taken a halfpenny ride on the tram, as this fare had been introduced specially to encourage people to use the cars for short distances. If he did, it would be appropriate, for he was going to interview the General Manager of the Tramways Department.

At one time all the business of the Town Council was carried on in the same building where the Council held its meetings. Now each department had to have its own headquarters, and the Tramway Offices, a large six-storey building at the corner of Bath Street and Renfield Street, had been built by the Corporation soon after they took over the tramway services from the private company. Under the stone canopy over the entrance was carved the city's Coat of Arms and the words 'GLASGOW CORPORATION TRAMWAYS'.

Mr Howe was met at the door by the commissionaire, dressed in the official green uniform of the department, and shown upstairs to the manager's office on the first floor to meet Mr James Dalrymple. He was introduced to a man of medium height and rather stocky, with stern eyes and a firm, determined mouth. A large moustache and short, pointed beard gave him an air of authority, and he had the reputation of being a *martinet* who would not tolerate any slackness or disobedience from any of the 4,400 men under him. Yet his views on transport matters were highly regarded, not only in Britain but also in many countries overseas, and his advice was asked on many occasions. When Mr Howe met him, he had just returned from a visit to the United States, having been specially invited by the Mayor of Chicago. Here was a man with an international reputation, and, according to Mr Howe, not ashamed to admit it.

> But Mr Dalrymple is a Scotsman. He could not be that and not be convinced that no other people in the world can do what Glasgow has done. That's Scots nature. They feel that way even towards England. It's human nature too, for haven't we been sending men to Glasgow for years to learn how that city does things? For Glasgow has made good on her tramways.

You may remember that the tram was an American invention. For an American to admit that a Scottish city probably possessed the finest tramway system in the world was a remarkable compliment to Glasgow, and not least to James Dalrymple. To many people at that time – even to some older people today – he was the man who did more than anyone else to gain Glasgow this reputation. Let us leave the two of them to discuss the running of the tramways, while we take a closer look at the life story of this remarkable man.

He was born in 1860 at a farm near the little Galloway town of Gatehouse-of-Fleet. Unlike John Young, however, he left the farm on leaving school at the age of fourteen, and became a clerk in the local branch of the Union Bank. In 1880 he was sent to their head office in Glasgow and made his home in the city for the rest of his life.

With his experience of banking, he was soon offered a post in the City Chamberlain's office. Here he became well known for the care he took over seeing the accounts were properly kept and for the way he could master any difficult financial problem that might crop up. In 1894 John Young asked him to join the new tramway department as their *accountant*. In due course he rose to become Mr Young's deputy, and in 1904, when Mr Young left Glasgow to take charge of the Metropolitan District Railway in London, Mr Dalrymple was *unanimously* chosen by the Corporation to succeed him as General

Manager. He remained there until he retired in 1926.

Let us go back to the start of his career with the tramways. One of his duties was to draw up a balance sheet at the end of each financial year to show the amount of money that the department had had to spend on wages and upkeep on the one hand, and the revenue taken in from fares paid by passengers on the other. Here is a short extract from the first year's account of 1894–95.

WAGES AND SALARIES	£	*s*	*d*
Office Staff	2,238	4	0
Drivers	22,037	6	0
Conductors	22,806	15	6
Night Foremen	779	15	10
Traffic Regulators	850	5	1
Trace Boys	1,838	2	9
Horse *Turners* and *Point Boys*	978	0	10
Total	£51,528	10	0

HORSING EXPENSES	£	*s*	*d*
Provender and *Litter*	67,242	5	2
Wages of Depot Foremen and Horsekeepers	23,136	12	4
Shoeing of horses	6,050	5	1
Veterinary treatment	648	3	0
Total	£97,077	5	7

However, during the same period the trams carried 57,104,647 passengers and the money collected in fares came to £221,600 10*s* 0*d*, so from the start the trams were making a profit. Some of this was used to pay for relaying track and for buying new cars. Some of it was put into a Reserve Fund to be used in the future when the great expense of changing over to electric traction had to be met. The rest was put aside every year to help to pay off the Tramway Debt. When the corporation started

James Dalrymple

to run the service in 1894, the money needed to do all the things mentioned at the end of Chapter 2 had to be borrowed from a special fund known as the Common Good. The tramways continued to make larger and larger profits every year and the contributions to the Common Good Fund grew accordingly, so that by 1917 the entire debt had been settled.

Have you noticed in the above accounts that it cost more to feed and stable the horses that pulled the trams than to pay the wages of all the men needed to run them on the streets? Also, the horses could not be locked away and forgotten when they were not needed, as one might do with a car or a bicycle. As we have seen, a large number of them could go down with some infectious illness, and so keep many of the trams out of service, possibly at a very busy time of the week like Saturday afternoon. Finally, although the trams were much superior to

Turning the horses at the terminus in St. Vincent Place for the return journey to Kelvinside

the ones the Company had formerly run, they were still very slow. More and more people might be tempted to use the local railway services, even if it meant having to walk some distance to the nearest station in preference to boarding a tram that passed along the street where they lived. The trams must be speeded up.

Already in other British cities, and in parts of Europe and America, electric power was being used to drive the trams. After visiting a number of these places, the Tramways Committee decided that the Glasgow Tramways must be electrified, but that they would start with one route as an experiment. One of of the 'white' routes – between Springburn and Mitchell Street – was chosen. Twenty-one electric cars were built specially for this purpose. They were single-deck and much longer than the horse cars, and had an entrance in the centre with a compartment on each side of it: one for those who wanted to smoke, and one for those who did not. The smokers did not

The first electric trams, 1898

have any glass in their compartment windows although there were blinds that could be pulled down in bad weather. Glasgow folk nicknamed them the 'But-and-Ben cars'. They resembled the American street-cars in appearance, and Mr Young may well have decided to have this type built after his visit to the United States about this time. They began running on 13 October 1898, and were so successful that it was decided to electrify the entire system as soon as possible. The last horse car was taken off the road at the end of April 1902.

For the second time within eight years, Mr Young and his staff had an enormous amount of work to do. The Corporation must have been glad to have a manager who did not easily get upset when things were difficult. First of all, they would need to relay with heavier rail more than eighty miles of track. They would have to erect poles on both sides of every street on which trams ran, in order to rig up the overhead electric wires carrying power to the cars. This power had to be fed into the wires at various points along each route, and had to be brought from the *generating station* in feeder cables laid underground in *ducts* along the centre of the street. Meanwhile, the horse trams had to continue running with all this upset going on round them. About four hundred new trams fitted with electrical equipment were built, many of them in the Corporation's own workshops at Coplawhill. Finally, at a cost of half-a-million pounds, a large generating station was built near Springburn, on the banks of the Forth and Clyde Canal. Pinkston Power Station was one of the largest in Europe when it was opened in 1901, and it was to continue to supply power to the tramways for over sixty years.

After all this worry and hard work, we can hardly be surprised to hear that John Young felt tired at the official lunch held to mark the opening of Pinkston. Perhaps he could not help feeling rather sorry that the horses, which he had taken

Coplawhill Works where most of Glasgow's trams were built. Part of it now houses the Museum of Transport

such care to select, were now to be sold off, and that the barns and stables, built less than ten years ago, would have to be put to other uses. At the same time, he knew that the electric cars could travel longer distances, and that within a few years the car lines would stretch out well beyond the city boundary into neighbouring towns and country villages. Under Mr Dalrymple this is what happened, but we have to remember that it was John Young who must take the credit for leaving the tramways in such fine shape for his successor to manage so well.

When James Dalrymple took charge of the tramways in 1904 the routes were already being extended not only within the city but to places that were at that time far beyond the city boundary. The horse car lines had been made to serve the needs of people who lived within a few miles of the city centre. The houses were there before the lines were laid. The electric car lines were now being pushed out into the country along roads

A tram in open country beyond the city limits

on which there were often very few houses. By 1910 Glasgow trams could be seen as far north as Killermont and Bishopbriggs, as far east as Baillieston Cambuslang and Uddingston, as far south as the two routes to Rouken Glen, and as far west as Paisley and Renfrew. The routes covered a distance of ninety-five miles altogether, and of these, thirty-eight miles were outside the Glasgow boundary.

These extensions were very costly, but in spite of this, the Department never failed to make a profit. The tramways earned more money every year as you can see from the statement below:

YEAR	ROUTES OPEN	NO. OF PASSENGERS	REVENUE
1901–02	51 milcs	163,678,190	£ 612,826– 2–4
1906–07	88 miles	224,063,098	£ 887,380–14–1
1912–13	98 miles	311,480,086	£1,007,652–17–6

Where did this extra money come from? Look at the number of passengers carried in the last year and compare it with the number shown for the earlier years. What James Dalrymple had done was to encourage more people to travel by tram. The fares were kept very cheap as you will see from the list of routes and fares on page 62–3. Even the longest journey – the fourteen miles from Uddingston to Paisley – costs no more than sevenpence, and few people would want to travel the whole distance. The normal fares for shorter stages came to something like this:

$\frac{1}{2}d$ for 1 mile	$2d$ for $4\frac{1}{2}$ miles
$1d$ for $2\frac{1}{2}$ miles	$2\frac{1}{2}d$ for $5\frac{3}{4}$ miles
$1\frac{1}{2}d$ for $3\frac{1}{2}$ miles	$3d$ for 7 miles

Cheap fares not only made people more ready to take the tram when formerly they might have walked. It began to take traffic away from the local railways, so that some stations such as Govan and Gorbals were closed, while train services on other lines were reduced. The trams were kept scrupulously clean and you never had to wait more than a few minutes for any car you might want. The single-deck cars had not been very popular with the public, and all the new cars that were built after the first twenty experimental ones for the Springburn route were double-deck cars with open tops. Mr Dalrymple soon had all but a few of them fitted with covered tops to make travel more pleasant in cold wet weather. Although he could not prevent people from smoking on the top deck, he insisted that smokers should take seats at the back of the car. Anyone spitting on the floor would be prosecuted and liable to a fine of forty shillings. This was more than a skilled workman or office clerk earned in a week, and, by making an example of a few offenders, the local Bailies succeeded in ending this disgusting practice that had caused such offence among tram passengers in the early days.

When the First World War broke out in 1914 thousands of men immediately volunteered to join the army. James Dalrymple turned part of the Tramway Offices into a recruiting centre, and sent out special cars plastered with posters urging men to join up. Nearly a thousand men from the various depots came forward in one day, and out of them was formed the 15th Highland Light Infantry, to be known as 'The Tramways Battalion'. To keep the services going when so many men were away he brought in women as drivers and conductors in their place. This was so successful that other towns in Britain did the same.

You will remember that his motto was 'We've still a long way to go.' During the war, shortage of steel and other raw materials made it impossible to extend the lines. However, when peace returned the tramways again pushed farther and farther out as new housing estates were built. Perhaps the most important thing he did was to urge the Corporation to take over the private companies who ran the trams in the Paisley district and between Coatbridge and Airdrie. Glasgow trams already ran to Paisley, so it was just a matter of taking their cars over and painting them in Glasgow colours. But a special two-mile length of track had to be made from Baillieston to Coatbridge to connect with their system. From 1923, it was possible to travel by one tram from Airdrie to Paisley, a distance of twenty-one miles – for twopence! Again, this was intended to draw people into Glasgow from these towns. It must have been successful, judging by the number of paper bags, with the names of bakers from Coatbridge printed on them, found littering a number of Glasgow's parks, on public holidays.

In the same year, the Corporation also took over the Glasgow Subway Railway, a 6½ mile underground line which ran in a continuous circle from the city centre to Govan and Partick, crossing the river on two occasions. Trains travelled in both directions and were hauled by a long steel cable rope. You can see the Subway route on the maps in the end covers. If you compare the 1896 map with the map of present-day Glasgow, you will see how the Subway really did cover a large part of the western side of the city, and even beyond the boundary, in its early days. It has never been extended, but it is now known as the Underground, and the trains are driven by electricity. Like the suburban railways, it had lost passengers once the electric trams appeared. But for James Dalrymple it might have had to close down, as the company who ran it were losing money on it every year.

James Dalrymple was certainly a hard *taskmaster* in his efforts to keep his huge department working efficiently, and it is not surprising to learn that he was never so well liked by his men as John Young had been. One of them, who had started as a conductor on the horse cars, put it like this: 'When Mr Young came to the depot, he would be sure to look in at the *bothy* for a chat with the men to see that everything was all right. But Mr Dalrymple always kept himself aloof.' Yet he had looked after them very well. Each man knew he was in a secure job with six days' paid holiday in the year. Moreover, if he took ill, the Tramway Employees' Friendly Society would pay him 15*s* each week as long as he was off work. For this benefit he had to pay sixpence each week and the Corporation added fourpence. When this scheme started there was no unemployment money or National Health Insurance. For a married man with a family to support, these benefits made a career as a tramwayman very attractive.

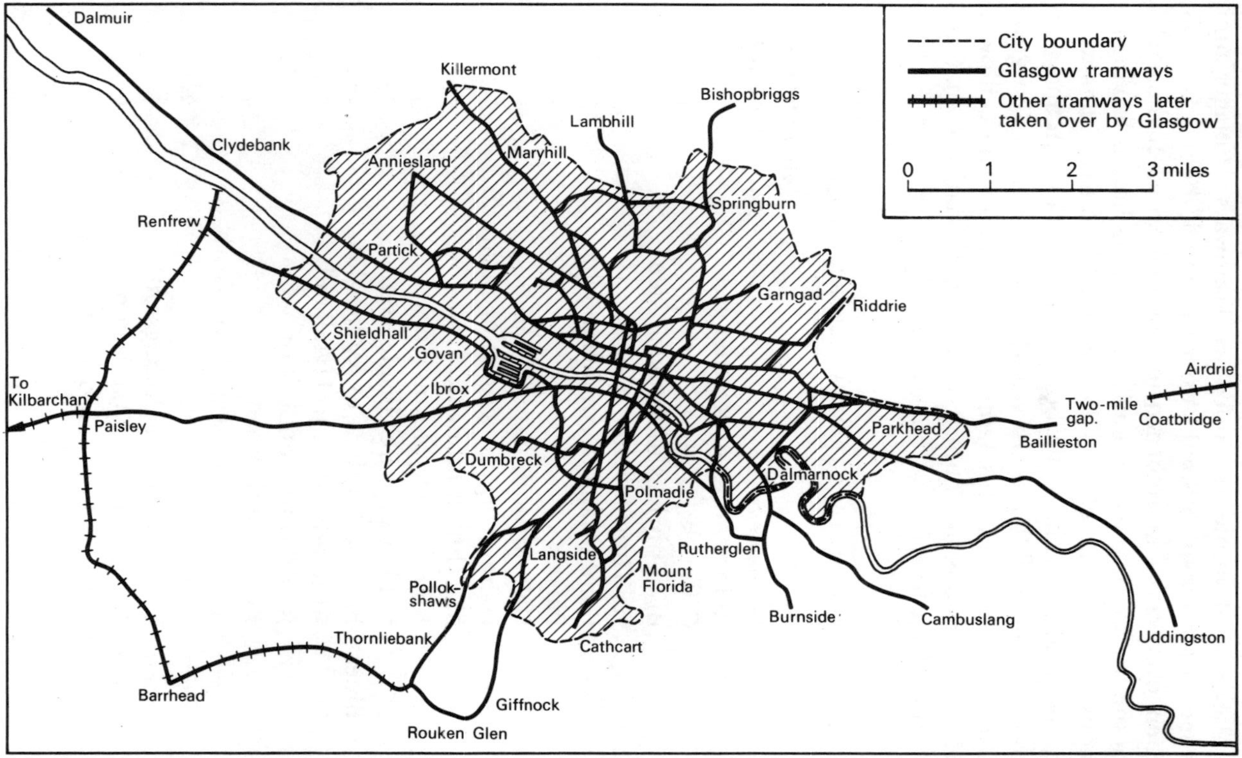

Glasgow tramway services 1914

James Dalrymple remained as Tramways Manager until 1926. After a visit to South America – to tell them how to run their tramways – he returned to Glasgow, which had been his home for so many years. Early in July 1934 he was leaving his house to attend a meeting – he could not bear to be idle – when he fell and broke his collarbone. Pneumonia set in and a few days later he died. For many years he had been one of Glasgow's leading citizens, but his family roots remained in Galloway. He was buried in the country cemetery of his native town, Gatehouse-of-Fleet.

GLASGOW'S TRAMWAY SERVICES IN 1914

Route Colour	*Destinations*	*Adult fare for full journey (pence)*
Red	Riddrie to Rouken Glen via Giffnock	4
	Bishopbriggs to Rouken Glen via Thornliebank	4
	Cambuslang to Anniesland via Partick	4
	Dalmuir to London Road	4½
	Dalmuir to Rutherglen or Burnside	5
	Maryhill to Trongate	1½
	Killermont to Mount Florida	3
	Battlefield to Kelvinside Avenue	2½
Blue	Botanic Gardens to Rutherglen	2½
	Alexandra Park to Hyndland	2
	Renfrew to Lambhill or Keppochhill Road	4
	Maryhill to Shawlands via Gorbals Cross	2½
Green	Paisley Cross to Uddingston	7
	Paisley Cross to Baillieston	6
	Springfield Road to Anniesland via Kelvinside	3½
	Whiteinch to Keppochhill Road	2

Yellow	Kirklee to Cathcart	3
	Jordanhill to Langside	3
	Paisley Road Toll to Riddrie via Bridgeton Cross	2½
	Paisley Road Toll to Mount Florida	1
White	Burnside to Springburn via Ruchill	4
	Springburn to Cathcart via Glasgow Cross	2½
	Polmadie to Garngad via Glasgow Cross	1½
	University to Dumbreck	2½
	Finnieston to Stobcross Ferry (No route colour – one small single-deck car provided this service)	½

5 *A Sail Down the Clyde*

Although Glasgow is a large, smoky, industrial city, you do not have to travel very far to reach some of the most famous beauty spots in Britain, like the Trossachs, Loch Lomond, and the Clyde Coast. As the River Clyde flows towards the sea it widens out into a great estuary, known as the Firth of Clyde. Here are found the large islands of Arran, Bute and the Great Cumbrae, and a number of sea lochs stretch like long fingers far into the rugged hills of Argyllshire. Ever since Henry Bell began the first steamboat service in Europe with his ship 'Comet' in 1812, it had been a habit for the average Glasgow family to sail down the Clyde in a river steamer and spend a holiday at one of the resorts that grew up around the Firth. Helensburgh, where Henry Bell was the Provost and had built the 'Comet' in the hope of attracting more visitors from Glasgow, was the earliest holiday town, and other coastal villages such as Dunoon, Largs and Millport soon became very popular. Rothesay, on the island of Bute, had been famous for its Royal Castle since the days of the Vikings, and more recently as the site of one of Scotland's first cotton mills. By the 1890s, it had become the greatest holiday centre for Glaswegians, especially during the second half of July – the Glasgow Fair Fortnight – when most of the factory workers had their annual holiday.

In order to see this famous place, and at the same time to learn something about the ships and shipbuilding yards that have made Glasgow and the Clyde renowned, let us take a day excursion 'doon the watter', as the Glasgow folk say. It is late in June 1906, and we turn to the back page of 'The Glasgow Herald' to find a suitable sailing. All the steamers leave from

POPULAR EXCURSIONS,
By Saloon Steamer
"ISLE OF ARRAN,"
DAILY from BRIDGE WHARF at 11 a.m.
Mondays and Thursdays............To LOCH STRIVEN.
Tuesdays and Fridays.............To KYLES OF BUTE.
Wednesdays and Saturdays........ROUND CUMBRAE.
Return Fares:—Steerage, 2/; Saloon, 2/6;
or Whole Day's Sail, with Dinner and Plain Tea, 4/6.

From the 'Glasgow Herald' of 28 June 1906

the Bridge Wharf on the Broomielaw, just downstream from the great new railway bridge that carries the lines of the Caledonian Railway into the Central Station.

We decide to take the 11 a.m. sailing by the 'Isle of Arran', and go on board in good time. She is a paddle steamer, like most of the Clyde steamers of that time, and has one funnel painted black with a white band near the top. She is one of a fleet of three ships owned by Captain William Buchanan, the others being named 'Isle of Bute' and 'Isle of Cumbrae'. We see a brass plate in her engine room that tells us that the 'Isle of Arran' is a ship of 312 tons, that she was built in 1892 by T.B. Seath and Co. of Rutherglen. (She was the last river steamer to be built at Rutherglen before the weir was built across the river at Glasgow Green, making further launches up-river impossible.)

There is a loud clang of bells from the ship's *telegraph*, as the captain signals the engineer to 'stand by'. The mooring ropes are cast off, the paddlewheels begin to churn up the water into thick foam, and the ship sets off down river. Both banks of the Clyde are lined with continuous quays and sheds. Several coastal steamers are tied up, busily loading cargoes for ports in England, Ireland or the West Highlands of Scotland. We notice the 'Tweed', a screw steamer whose funnel is painted the same as that of the 'Isle of Arran'. She is bound for Bristol. The 'Vulture' of the Burns line has brought in passengers overnight from Belfast, while the 'Shamrock' of the Laird line, with her attractive red, white and black funnel, is preparing to sail that evening for Dublin. A little farther on

Steamers leaving the Broomielaw about the turn of the century

we come to the berths of ocean-going ships and the great docks lying parallel to the river: the Queen's Dock to the north anc Prince's Dock to the south. Passenger *liners* and *tramp steamer* are tied up in one or other of them. Here is the 'Numidian of the Allan line, bound for Montreal, the 'City of Corinth of the Ellerman line, just arrived from Calcutta, the Clan liner 'Clan Lamont' with a cargo of fruit from Cape Town, an unusual ship with large *derricks* but no masts and a very tall blu funnel, the 'Cyclops'. Her trade is mainly with China and th Far East, and we can see several *lascar* seamen on board wh serve as firemen in ships sailing in tropical seas. There is als a passenger liner with three large black funnels lying alongside the quay at Finnieston. This is the Anchor liner 'Columbia and she is ready to sail with a full *complement* of passengers fo New York. Many emigrants from Britain to America an Canada will be among them, hoping for a better life in th prairie regions now being opened up in those lands.

These are all steamships, but there are still to be seen th

Crossing the river by ferry. A Hopper is in the background

masts and rigging of several *windjammers*, though sailing ships are becoming fewer every year. They are still very popular on the grain routes from Australia. Here is the four-masted 'Loch Ness', unloading wheat at Meadowside Quay after a voyage from Melbourne. Over at Prince's Dock, a similar vessel, the 'Glenshee' is preparing to set sail for New Zealand. Their crews must have many a gripping story to tell of the severe weather conditions and mountainous seas they have to meet as they round Cape Horn on their homeward voyages.

Now we hear the incessant hammering of the *riveters* as we near the shipbuilding yards. We note the names of some of them as we sail past. Our ship has reduced speed so as not to cause too much wash while passing the launching berths, which are placed at a sharp angle to the river in case the newly launched vessel should strike the opposite bank. Some of the world's greatest ships have come from these yards: Harland and Wolff Ltd, Alexander Stephen and Sons Ltd, Fairfield Co. Ltd, are on the south side in the then separate Burgh of Govan.

On the north side we can see the yards of D. and W. Henderson, Barclay, Curle and Co. Ltd, and John Brown and Co. Ltd, of Clydebank. We are keeping a very sharp lookout for the last one, as they have just launched a new ship of 33,000 tons for the Cunard Line. She is called 'Lusitania', and we see her being fitted out in the basin alongside the yard. With her four red and black funnels, her ultra-modern passenger accommodation and her six powerful steam turbines, she is expected to win back for Britain the Blue Riband of the Atlantic, an award given to the ship making the fastest crossing, and at that time held by Germany. (The 'Lusitania' was to become even more famous during the First World War when she was sunk off the Irish Coast by a German submarine in 1915. More than 1,000 people were drowned.)

The 'Lusitania'

We now leave the Glasgow area, as the river winds along the foot of the Kilpatrick Hills, past the great landmark of Dumbarton Rock, and on towards the industrial area around Port Glasgow and Greenock. Away to the north and west we get a foretaste of the Scottish Highlands in the craggy hills and peaks beyond the Holy Loch and at the head of Loch Long. The gentler hills of Cowal stretch away to the south from above Dunoon, as the river takes a great right-angled bend and becomes the Firth.

One of the famous 'puffers'

We notice some of the ships that pass us on their way up river to Glasgow. They are mainly small vessels: one or two hoppers which carry away the silt brought up from the river bed by the dredgers in order to keep the channel clear for ships; a coaster with a cargo of granite from Bonawe, near Oban; Glasgow Corporation's sludge steamer 'Dalmuir', with her grey hull and yellow funnel; and one of the well-known steam *lighters*, nicknamed 'puffers', which carry all kinds of cargoes, and can be found in all parts of Scotland's West Coast. They are short, well-rounded ships, with the funnel near the stern, a mast and derrick on the *forecastle* and a large hold *amidships*. Neil Munro made them famous in his stories of the 'Vital Spark' and her wily, good-natured captain, Para Handy. Perhaps you have read of the exploits of him and his crew, which first appeared in a Glasgow evening newspaper in 1901.

Route of the Isle of Arran

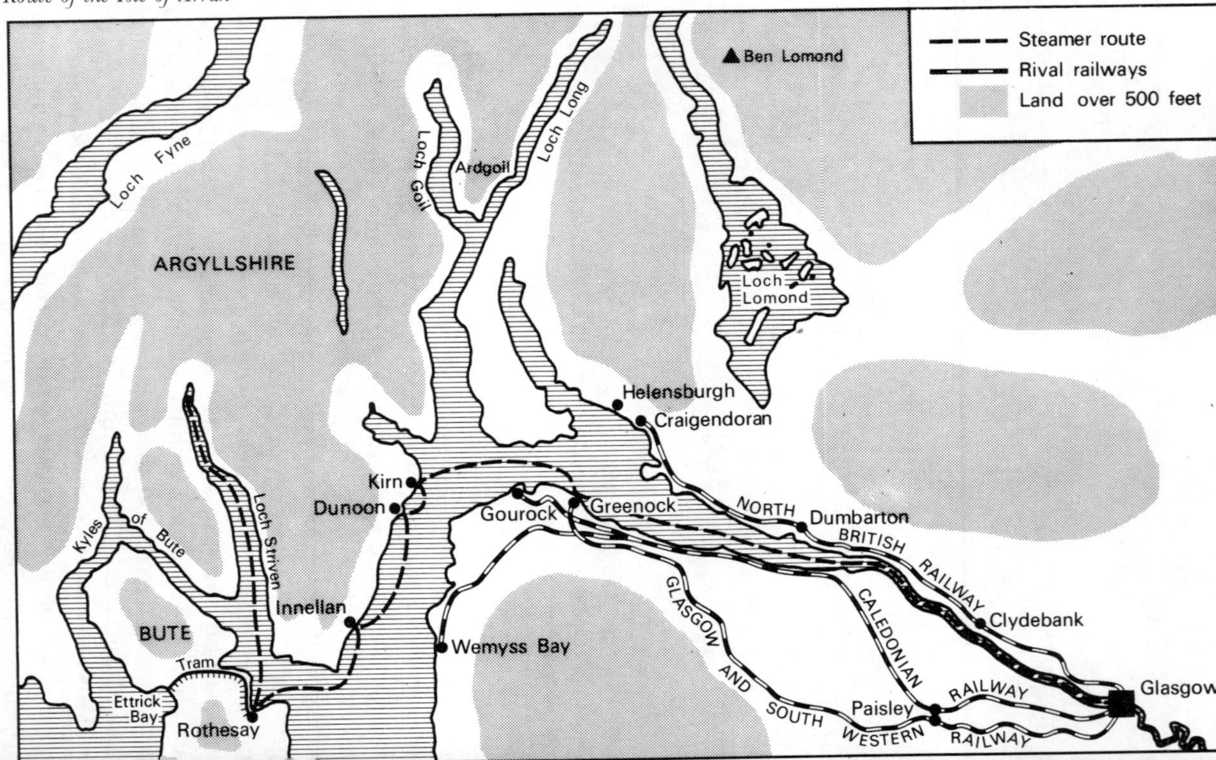

Yet, apart from one aged paddle steamer, the 'Benmore', owned by Captain Buchanan's great rival, Captain John Williamson, we have not seen another river steamer, and we may wonder how people manage to get to the coast towns. We shall soon find the answer. At that time three rival railway companies ran trains between Glasgow and the upper Clyde ports: the Caledonian to Gourock and Wemyss Bay, the Glasgow and South Western to Greenock (Prince's Pier), and the North British to a point east of Helensburgh called Craigendoran. (You can see them on the map.) It was quicker and more pleasant to go by train to one of these *railheads* and board a ship there for the rest of the journey to Dunoon, Rothesay or farther afield. As each company wanted to attract the most passengers, they began, about 1890, to run their own steamers, each fleet having distinctive names and colours. The Caledonian boats were like steam yachts, having black hulls, white paddleboxes, pink saloon panels and buff yellow funnels. They were called after titled ladies, such as 'Duchess of Hamilton' and 'Marchioness of Lorne'. The Glasgow and South Western boats had grey hulls and red and black funnels and were named after Roman gods, like 'Jupiter' and 'Neptune'. The North British fleet had black paddleboxes and red funnels with black tops and a narrow white band between the black and red. They were named after novels and characters of Sir Walter Scott, like 'Waverley' and 'Lucy Ashton'. Of course rival steamers would race one another to reach the next pier ahead of the other, and the local inhabitants, especially schoolboys, would support their favourite – Caley, Sou'West, or N.B. – as if it were a football team. When we call at Prince's Pier, only the 'Minerva' is there, as it is a slack period in the day. Perhaps on our way back we shall see some excitement.

Some passengers have joined us at Greenock for an afternoon sail on the Firth, and others will board or disembark at Kirn, Dunoon and Innellan where the ship also calls. We can now see the peaks of Arran away down the Firth, and a splendid panorama of steep-sided hills and lochs appears on our right as the 'Isle of Arran' rounds the point at Toward Lighthouse

Smoke from the funnel could be unpleasant for passengers on the deck of The G & S.W Steamer 'Minerva'

and sails into Rothesay Bay. To make the sail even more enjoyable, a *trio* of musicians – piano, violin and *melodeon* – are playing Scots tunes and other popular airs. One of them occasionally asks us for a collection in a small velvet bag which he carries.

The 'Isle of Arran' in Rothesay Bay

At 2.30 we reach Rothesay Pier, a long wharf built out in front of the harbour where six steamers can berth at one time. The holiday season is only beginning, but a small crowd is waiting to join the ship for an afternoon cruise to the head of Loch Striven. There you could imagine yourself in a Norwegian *fiord* rather than merely thirty miles from the centre of Glasgow. However, we shall spend the two hours ashore in Rothesay. We can walk along the promenade of the west shore, listen to a concert at the bandstand on a spot now occupied by the Winter Gardens, climb to the top of the woods behind the town for a view of the bay and the Cowal hills, or – a great attraction – take the electric tram across the island to a wonderful sandy beach called Ettrick Bay. The single-deck cars have open sides and crossbench seats, and are known as 'toastracks'. On a fine day, this five-mile trip is most enjoyable, and in the height of summer the long cars are so packed with holidaymakers that the local people who want to travel shorter distances to their homes find it easier to walk.

The time passes quickly, and the ship's siren warns us that it is nearly 4.45 and time to sail. The 'Isle of Arran' swings away from the pier as the telegraph rings Full Speed Ahead. When we reach Innellan, we can see the reason for this haste. The evening rush hour on the Firth has started. Between 4 o'clock and 4.10 three trains have left Glasgow, and the three steamers which were impatiently awaiting their arrival at Greenock, Gourock and Craigendoran respectively have now left Dunoon and are racing towards Innellan. Each leaves a great white wake of water churned up by its paddles, and dense clouds of black smoke roll out from the funnels as the firemen try to coax an extra turn of speed out of their ship. As they pass us, the 'Mercury' seems to be winning, but the 'Duchess of Fife', a much newer boat, forges ahead suddenly to make the pier first. The 'Talisman' is some way behind, but is in no hurry, as she is timed to sail a few minutes behind the others. (Can you work out to which companies these steamers belonged?)

A race for Kirn Pier between a Caledonian and a G & S.W. Steamer

These daily races are most exciting, and the steamers give an excellent service to the coast towns, but it is very wasteful, and the companies are losing money. Captain James Williamson, who has spent many years in the steamer trade and is now in charge of the Caledonian boats, is quite clear about this: 'Much of the service is *superfluous* and needless, the sole advantage derived from the running of three steamers where one would serve being to afford the public a choice of route.' This, in fact, is what happened only a few years later when the companies agreed to co-operate with one another and to sell some of their ships.

Off Gourock, at what is called 'The Tail of the Bank', we meet the 'Columbia', all set for her voyage across the Atlantic. The sun is beginning to set over the hills to the west as we make our way upriver past the silent shipyards and quays. Work is over for the day. Finally, we leave the 'Isle of Arran', with regret, at the Broomielaw. It is more than nine hours since we set off. We have had a most enjoyable day's sailing, including an excellent lunch and tea. The total cost has been four shillings and sixpence!

6 *The Festive Season*

Today Glasgow is a very bright and gay place at Christmas. The shop windows have special displays to tempt the shoppers looking for presents to give to their families and friends. People come from towns and villages many miles from the city not only to visit the big stores but to see the wonderful displays of lights and illuminated *tableaux* in the main streets, and especially in George Square, where the front of the City Chambers is floodlit. Christmas trees with their coloured lights can be seen in the windows of most houses. It is now the custom to draw back the curtains of the window at this time so that everyone can enjoy the sight of the lit trees and feel that the Christmas season is here once again.

But if we were to go back to the period around the turn of the century, the time we have been looking at in this book, we would find things very different at Christmas. Many people still felt that the celebration of Christmas was wrong. At the time of the Reformation in the middle of the sixteenth century the great Scottish reform leader, John Knox, and his supporters had declared that the religious festivals of the Catholic Church, such as Christmas, Easter and Whitsun, should be abolished in the new Church of Scotland. Two hundred years later, most Scots people still thought like this, although towards the end of the nineteenth century there were some signs of a change of heart, especially if there were children in the home. The author, J.J. Bell, who was brought up in the West End of the city, tells us:

> Christmas meant nothing to the working people, unless as a reminder of the approach of the New Year. To many

> middle-class people it was still a matter almost for resentment, since they regarded it as just one more Anglified *innovation*. There were middle-class homes like my own, in which, as Christmas drew near, the house became – amiably withal – divided against itself. My father's people, with their old-fashioned ideas and prejudices, did not 'hold with' Christmas; my mother's people, with their new notions and *prepossessions*, were all for it.

In some homes, holly and mistletoe might be put up for Christmas week, and perhaps paper chains and imitation Chinese lanterns, each with a lighted candle stuck in its base, might be strung across the room. The postman probably noticed that his bag was a little heavier on Christmas Day as he delivered a few Christmas cards and presents, but there was no need then to bring in extra helpers to handle the mail. Many families never knew what a Christmas card looked like. J.J. Bell's father even used to boast that he had never received one in his life.

For most people 25 December, unless it happened to fall on a Sunday, was a normal working day. Banks, insurance companies, and some offices that did business with England, would have a day's holiday, but the markets, the factories and the shops would open as usual. Schools might be closed for the day, if the *School Board* allowed it, but the children had to be back at their desks on the following morning. (Fancy having only one or two days' holiday at Christmas!) Bank clerks used to enjoy spending Christmas morning visiting the big city stores. There was no letup even for Father Christmas in the toy department. He was expected to stay in his Toyland Grotto, as the busiest week of the whole year was the one between Christmas and New Year, when most of the presents were bought.

Perhaps the first sign that times were changing was a notice on the front page of 'The Glasgow Herald' of Monday, 24 December 1906:

> The gradual movement which has taken place in public *sentiment* during recent years towards observing the Christ-

The shopwalker stands ready to assist customers at Pettigrew and Stephens' Grand Staircase

mas Season, if not the day, has seemed to meet with general approval, and to give the lead to traders generally (believing that both Christmas and New Year can well be kept)

Pettigrew and Stephens Ltd.

have decided this year, and for the future, to free their employees from attendance on Christmas Day and

OBSERVE IT AS A HOLIDAY

The warehouse will therefore be closed TOMORROW THE 25th.

Pettigrew and Stephens Ltd was, and is, one of Glasgow's largest department stores, and within the next few years most of the others were following their example.

Yet we must not think that there was no enjoyment or festivity in Glasgow at this time. The New Year was the great holiday season in Scotland as most people were on holiday on 1 and 2 January. This was the time when family reunions were held, and people went to parties in each other's houses. This, rather than Christmas, was the time for giving and receiving presents. In the city there was always plenty of entertainment after your gifts had been bought: concerts in the St Andrews Hall and the City Hall, football matches, and a large number of theatres.

Let us imagine that it is New Year's Eve – or Hogmanay as it is better known – of 1913. The weather has been very cold over Christmas, but it is becoming milder now, and the frost and snow is rapidly disappearing. The streets are crowded with last-minute shoppers. It seems that more people have money to spend than in previous years, as there is full employment in the shipyards along the Clyde, and in the factories and foundries that supply their needs. Much of this prosperity is due to the fact that the Government is worried at the rapid rise of the German Navy, and is determined to equip the Royal Navy with the most modern and powerful warships. Many of these naval vessels, including the 'Dreadnought' battleships, are being built in Clyde yards, and during the past year nearly one third of all ships built in Britain have been launched on

An artistic menu board painted by Mackintosh for Miss Cranston's Willow Tearooms in 1911

the Clyde. For many families this is going to be the most enjoyable New Year they can remember.

For those able to afford to buy more expensive gifts, the advertisements in the newspapers sound very tempting, like this one by a firm that specialises in travelling goods:

	s d
Umbrellas	from 10 6
Writing case	8 6
Week-end kit bag	17 6
Hide suit case	14 6
Cabin case	30 0
Travelling rug	10 6
Slippers (folding in case)	5 6
Shaving mirror	2 6
Thermos flask	6 6

How much would these articles cost today? Certainly much more than they did in 1913. However, if we remember that at that time a skilled tradesman, with a wife and family to support, rarely earned more than 40*s* per week, we can see that prices were not as low as we might think.

During the holiday period, great crowds will make their way to the football grounds, to support their favourite team. Some of the best-known Scottish teams are from Glasgow – Queen's Park, Clyde, Third Lanark, Partick Thistle, and the two deadly rivals, Rangers and Celtic. Since the beginning of the century, these big teams have spent large sums of money in

Newspaper seller in Gordon Street

Queen's Park, a well-known football team at this time

improving their grounds. No longer is it enough to expect the spectators to stand on flat ground around the field. Now, the field is surrounded by massive terracing, rising as much as fifty feet from the ground, with seats under a covered grandstand at one side of the field. Rangers built Ibrox Stadium in 1898, followed soon after by Celtic at Parkhead and Queen's Park's magnificent Hampden Park, the largest football ground in Britain. Sometimes nearly 100,000 spectators will attend a big game. Some of them will never forget that terrible day at Ibrox eleven years earlier, on Saturday 5 April 1902. On a brilliant sunny day, 75,000 people had come to see Scotland play England in the annual International Game, the largest crowd ever known at a match:

> A simple incident prefaced it. A corner kick at the west goal had been given. The packed masses on the terracing surged and swayed in their anxiety to follow the issue of it; the structure strained and creaked under the weight and agitation of the mass it supported; and then a wide portion of

The Ibrox Football Disaster, 1902

> it near the top fell in, carrying with it the luckless people who stood there.

The unfortunate spectators were hurled to the ground forty feet below. Every ambulance in the city was rushed to Ibrox and every hospital in Glasgow did what it could to attend to the injured, who numbered several hundred. Twenty-three people lost their lives in this accident. Yet the game continued as before. One spectator arrived home after the game to find his wife almost sick with worry, on hearing the newsboys' shouts of 'Ibrox disaster – many dead'. He, and many others, had not realised that anything serious had happened!

Fortunately, accidents of this kind are very rare. As a result of the Ibrox disaster, the terracing in the big football grounds was made much stronger.* Next to International Games, the greatest crowds would usually be found at the Final for the Scottish Cup. Since 1904 this has been played at Hampden Park. Excitement among the crowd would reach fever pitch, especially if the 'Old Firm' – Rangers and Celtic – met in the final round. Unfortunately, enthusiasm, if not checked, could give way to hooliganism. On 17 April 1909 a riot took place at Hampden Park during a Cup Final replay between Rangers and Celtic. Both goalposts were uprooted and set on fire along with fencing surrounding the pitch. A section of the crowd attacked police, firemen, and even ambulance men trying to assist those people injured in the fighting. Over a hundred people, including forty-five policemen had to be treated in hospital. The Scottish Cup was not awarded in that year.

Although there was no radio or television in those days there was plenty of entertainment in the long winter evenings. In every middle-class sitting room you would see a piano, and musical evenings, when almost every guest would play or sing, with the others joining in the choruses, were held regularly. The gramophone, with its large horn, as seen on the label of His Master's Voice records, was also very popular, and made

*However, on 2 January 1971 another terrible disaster occurred in which 66 lives were lost.

it possible to play over and over again one's favourite songs or orchestral music, so enjoyed at a theatre or concert hall.

Above all, there were the theatres. If we look at a newspaper on the last day of 1913 we see that we have a wide variety of shows to choose from. There are pantomimes, musical comedies, *vaudeville* shows in which some of the leading entertainers in Britain will be appearing, and, at the Savoy Theatre, even a *tango* competition in which the audience is invited to take part. More serious drama is being presented at the Royalty Theatre, where for the past four years, the Glasgow Repertory Theatre Company has put on plays, some of which were being performed for the first time. Glasgow audiences are known to be very *discriminating*, and very often a play or musical show will be tried out in Glasgow before being taken to London.

But it is the music hall and the pantomime that most people will flock to on this New Year's Eve. Many of the greatest comedians in Britain first made their name in one or other of Glasgow's theatres. The most famous of all was Harry Lauder, who with his crooked stick and tartan bonnet and his rich, genial humour was to delight audiences throughout the world, and, for better or worse, make people think of him as a typical Scotsman. He was, moreover, a very fine singer, and many of his songs such as 'I love a lassie' and 'Roamin' in the Gloamin'', are still very popular today. These and others were first heard at Glasgow pantomimes in the early years of the century.

As it happens, Glasgow's most famous song, written at this time, was not one of Harry Lauder's. A young Dundee comedian, Will Fyffe, had written a number which he hoped Harry Lauder would sing. However, Will Fyffe was asked to appear at short notice at Glasgow's Pavilion Theatre and became famous overnight by singing the song himself. It was called 'I Belong to Glasgow'.

As well as the theatres, there are also a number of cinemas, or 'picture theatres' as they were then called. The silent movie picture industry was flourishing in America by 1913, although another fifteen years would pass before a sound track was

Harry Lauder, in one of his famous character sketches

added. Meanwhile, sub-titles are used to tell the story, and the background music is provided by a pianist or group of musicians playing in front of the screen. Some picture theatres have a full orchestra which plays selections between the films. The Picture House (now the Gaumont) in Sauchiehall Street, has a Palm Court where people can have tea and meet their friends. The La Scala, on the opposite side of the street, has a Japanese Tea Room, where you can take tea and still enjoy the film at the same time. Admission prices range from sixpence for the front stalls to one and sixpence for special box seats. To encourage you to go regularly, some films are shown as serials, one part each week. 'Who will marry Mary?' Part 3, is on the bill this New Year.

As midnight approaches, large crowds begin to gather around the Tolbooth at Glasgow Cross. The Old Year is played out with suitable music played on a *carillon* of bells in the Tolbooth Tower. As the clock strikes midnight, heralding in 1914, there is much cheering and hand shaking among the crowds as they make their way to *first-foot* their friends. People believe it is lucky if the first person to cross the threshold has dark hair, and he, or she, must carry some gift for the household – usually shortbread and a rich dark cake made of currants, raisins, almonds, ginger, cinnamon and Jamaica pepper, known as Black Bun. On their way they hear the factory hooters saluting the New Year helped from far down the river by the sirens of ships in dock.

The next two days will see Glasgow on holiday. For those keen on sport there is the annual New Year game between Rangers and Celtic, held this year at Parkhead (Celtic won 4–0). At mid-day, the annual performance of Handel's 'Messiah' will be given in St Andrews Hall by the Glasgow Choral and Orchestral Union. The soldiers stationed at Maryhill Barracks are roused by pipers playing 'A Guid New Year to Ane an A'', and can look forward to a day free from parades or drills. A number of churches hold short thanksgiving services.

One newspaper, commenting on the scene, remarks: 'The continued prosperity in trade has brought with it more spend-

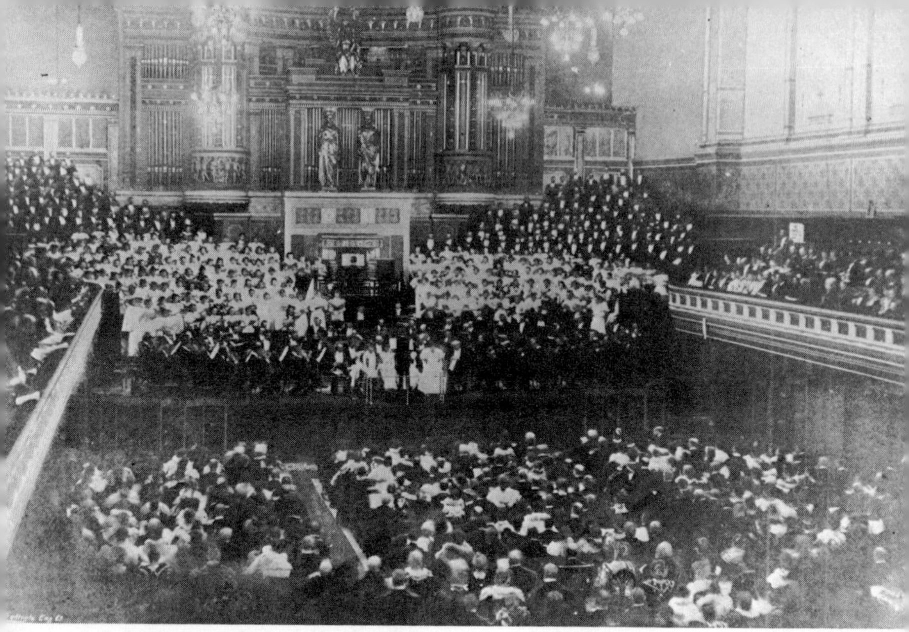

A performance of Handel's 'Messiah' in St. Andrews Hall

ing money and banished almost entirely the depression which overshadowed the occasion a few years ago. The city never bore a more festive appearance.'

Eight months later Britain declared war on Germany. The results of that war brought heavy unemployment to Glasgow's shipyards and other heavy industries. It is not surprising that people who knew the city in 1914 often tell us that things have never been the same since that time.

How do we know?

In this book a great deal has been said of the work done by Glasgow Corporation in providing so many essential services for its citizens. The Minutes of the Council Meetings and the Annual Reports and Accounts of each department are carefully preserved in the City Archives, and are invaluable in providing detailed information on what the various departments did and how much it cost them. In the period we have been looking at, a great number of books were written on this topic, showing how great an interest was taken by the public in municipal affairs at this time. Three of these are particularly useful: 'Glasgow, its Municipal Organisation and Administration' was written in 1896 by Sir James Bell, who had been Lord Provost for the previous six years; 'Municipal Enterprises' (1904), and 'Municipal Glasgow' (1914) were published as handbooks by the Corporation. Mr Howe's impressions of Glasgow can be found partly in his book, 'European Cities at Work' and partly in an article he wrote for an American journal, 'Scribner's Magazine' in July 1906.

For the other parts of the book, not directly concerned with the Corporation's work, the newspapers of the day provided a great deal of information, not only about what was happening but also as to what people felt about these happenings; for example, a visitor's comments on the smoke menace on the Clyde steamers, how a new show was received in a local theatre, and the angry feelings of one reader on the question of whether Christmas should be observed more widely in Scotland (this was in 1906).

Above all, as this book deals with a period still within the memory of elderly people, personal opinions were most valuable in trying to recreate a picture of a past age. One person consulted was a man in his nineties, who had started as a conductor on the horse trams in 1896 under John Young. The spectator at the Ibrox Football Disaster was the author's grandfather.

These are some of the sources from which history can be written. Fortunately there are many very readable and easily obtained books for you to follow up this brief story of this great, fascinating city. Here are some suggestions. The best general account, with a large number of illustrations, is 'The Second City' by C. A. Oakley (Blackie, 1967). A shorter book, showing how the city has spread over former farmland, is 'Glasgow, A Concise History' by John R. Kellett (Blond, 1967). Another general history is 'Glasgow' by J. M. Reid (Batsford, 1956). 'The Heart of Glasgow' by Jack House (Hutchinson, 1965), confines itself to the older part of the city, but is an excellent guide to present and former buildings in almost every street, with many stories of notable people and incidents connected with them. For a picture of the late nineteenth and early twentieth century Glasgow based on personal memories, you should read 'The Brave Days' by Neil Munro (Blackwood, 1931), and 'I Remember' by J. J. Bell (Porpoise Press, 1932). They were written many years ago, but you will find them in a public library. You should also enjoy reading 'The Para Handy Tales' by Neil Munro (Blackwood, 1963; referred to in Chapter 5), and J. J. Bell's 'Wee Macgreegor' (Chambers, n.e. 1933), the escapades of a lively young Glasgow schoolboy who was always up to some mischief. Both these characters first appeared in Glasgow evening newspaper short stories around 1900. The full story of the tramways is told in C. A. Oakley's 'The Last Tram', published by Glasgow Corporation to commemorate the close-down in 1962. Many books have been written about the Clyde river steamers. Captain James Williamson's 'The Clyde Passenger Steamer' (1904) is an account of the history of steamships on the Clyde down to 1901, by a man who helped to make that history. 'The Golden Years of the Clyde Steamers', by Alan J. S. Paterson (David and Charles, 1969), deals with the period from 1889 to 1914, when the rivalry between the various railway companies' steamers was very keen. Both these subjects have their enthusiasts, and booklets and magazines on these are regularly published by the Scottish Tramway Museum Society and the Clyde River Steamer Club.

The Mitchell Library in Glasgow has a room set aside specially for books on the city. There are very fine exhibits at the three main Corporation musuems: Kelvingrove Art Galleries, built for the 1901 Exhibition; The Old Glasgow Museum on Glasgow Green; and the Museum of Transport, housed in part of the former Coplawhill Tramway Works, where most of Glasgow's horse and electric cars were built.

Finally, if possible, try to visit the Crich Tramway Museum, high up in the moorlands near Matlock in Derbyshire. Here can be seen a varied collection of trams, including six from Glasgow. During summer weekends, visitors can travel along a three-quarter mile length of track on cars powered from overhead electric wires, and experience what a tram journey was like in former times.

A Glasgow 'White' tram, restored to its original condition, now running at Crich Tramway Museum, Derbyshire

Things to do

1. Did your town ever have a tramway service? If so, try to find out (from people who remember it) where the lines were laid and along what routes the trams ran. Find out when the tram services closed and see if there was a closing ceremony as in Glasgow. (Your local library may have a file copy of a local paper that would describe when and why the trams were withdrawn.)
2. Look for any features in the town that would act as clues to discovering a former tramway. Rosettes on the walls of buildings, poles that once carried tram wires, former depot buildings with possibly tram tracks still in position, are good evidence of this. This type of study is now being called 'industrial archaeology'.
3. If you live in a burgh or city, find the names of the three councillors who represent your ward. In what order are they due to retire? How long has each been a member of the Town Council?
4. Find out the names of the Provost (Mayor), Bailies (Magistrates), Treasurer and Dean of Guild (Planning Officer) of your town. If you live in England, the officials will be called by the names in brackets. How many Committees does your Council have? See if you can find the names of the Town Clerk, the Chamberlain (Borough Treasurer) and at least four other important council officials.
5. Try to attend a meeting of the Town Council (this might best be arranged through your school).
6. If Mr Howe were to visit Glasgow today, make a list of some of the great changes he would find as compared with his visit in 1905.
7. Hold a mock Council debate. Appoint a Provost and Conveners for one or two committees. Discuss how some present problems in the town might be dealt with, and what the Council should do about them.
8. If you have the chance to sail down the Clyde from Glasgow to Rothesay, make a note of the changes that have taken place since the 'Isle of Arran' trip of 1906, as related in Chapter 5.

9. Ask your art teacher to tell you about Charles Rennie Mackintosh. If possible, try to visit a building in Glasgow designed by him. (Glasgow School of Art, Queen's Cross Church, Scotland Street School are three examples. The distinctive first and second floor frontage at the west end of Daly's Department Store in Sauchiehall Street were once part of Miss Cranston's Willow Tearooms.)
10. Make a list of songs made famous by Sir Harry Lauder – with help from your grandparents and their friends. Why do you think they have remained so popular?
11. Write an account of an important football game you have attended, stressing any exciting moments in the game.
12. Make a list of traditional New Year customs in Scotland. See if you can find a recipe for making Black Bun.
13. Make up an imaginary argument between two people living around 1906. One wants Christmas to be celebrated more widely in Scotland, the other is against any change.
14. Find out how people liked to spend their evenings at home before the days of radio and television.
15. You may have noticed that there was no Education Committee in Glasgow Corporation in 1904 (see p. 41). This was because, until 1918, schools came under special School Boards based on parishes. Find out which School Board controlled the schools in your area – you may find its name carved in stone on the building.
16. Make a collection, from newspapers and magazines, of photographs and drawings showing views of Glasgow and the Clyde in the days before 1914. Arrange them methodically under suitable headings in an album: for example, Going to Work, Shopping, Travel, Entertainments, On Holiday.
17. If you have, or can borrow, a portable tape recorder, arrange to visit some elderly people and ask them questions about town life as they remember it sixty or more years ago. Record your interviews and keep the tape as a valuable historical record.

Glossary

accountant, official responsible for all money taken in or paid out
amidships, the middle section of a ship between the bow and the stern
aqueduct, bridge with a channel along the top for carrying water
to ascertain, to find out
asphalt, a tarry substance obtained from natural oil and used for surfacing roads
bothy, place where workmen can rest when off duty
burgh, town that has obtained the right to elect its own council to run its affairs (spelt 'borough' in England)
carillon, set of bells in a tower, designed to play a tune
celebrity, a famous person
civic, concerned with the city
commodious, roomy
complement, number required to fill the accommodation in a ship
constituency, district represented by a Member of Parliament
contaminated, infected with some harmful substance
conveyance, any vehicle which carries passengers or goods
council houses, dwelling houses belonging to a town or county council, which are let to tenants
crèche, public nursery for very young children (French = manger)
deadlock, complete standstill, inability to come to an agreement
depot, building used for storing public transport vehicles
derrick, swivelling crane, with an adjustable arm, usually found on ships
to discriminate, to be able to judge the value of something
duct, tube laid under the road surface for carrying an electric cable
dux, head boy
eminence, great importance
era, period in history clearly marked off from those before and after it
fiord, deep inlet of the sea, with steep-sided hills rising from its shores
first-foot, the first person to enter a stranger's house at New Year

flanged, having a projecting rim on its outer side
fogey, an old man, out of touch with modern ideas
forecastle, short raised deck at the bow of a ship
generating station, building where electric power is produced
hallmark, distinguishing feature that identifies something
hansom, two-wheeled, horse-drawn cab, in which the driver sat up at the back
to heckle, to question a speaker sharply and persistently
indissoluble, not able to be set free
innovation, new idea
investor, person who lends money to a private company or a public corporation, so that he may be paid interest on it regularly
kindergarten, infant school
lascar, sailor from India or the East Indies
lease, right to take control of some property or service for a fixed period of time in return for paying an agreed sum of money
legislation, the making of laws, usually by Parliament
lighter, small, flat-bottomed boat, carrying all kinds of bulk cargo.
liner, passenger or cargo ship sailing between Britain and foreign ports on a regular service
litter, straw bedding for horses
mace, an ornate metal club, brought in at all official corporation meetings to show that business can begin
martinet, one who keeps strict discipline
melodeon, small accordion
municipal, relating to the public affairs of a city
point boys, boys stationed at tramway junctions in busy streets to alter the points, when needed, with a long metal lever
postillion, man who rides the leading horse of a team drawing a vehicle
prepossessions, fixed ideas
provender, food for animals
radical, determined to change the present methods of government.
railhead, station at the end of a railway line
rates, money paid by property owners to a local council for the upkeep of public services
to remit, to send to a higher court, without passing judgment
reservoir, man-made lake for storing water
riveters, men who bolt together the metal plates of a ship
Royal Burgh, burgh that received its charter from a Scottish king before the Treaty of Union of 1707
School Board, elected committee of prominent local people who were responsible for the schools in their particular district

sentiment, feeling
serge, a kind of worsted cloth
sewage, refuse, waste matter, carried away by drains
sludge, solid material left after sewage has been purified.
suburbs, residential areas on the fringe of the city
superflous, more than is needed
tableaux, groups of figures forming a picture
tango, a South American dance, very popular in ballroom dancing
taskmaster, person who demands high standards from those working for him
telegraph, electric apparatus by which the ship's captain signals instructions from the bridge to the engine room
tenement, large building, three or more storeys high, divided into a large number of separate dwelling houses
tiers, rows of seats rising one behind the other
trace boys, boys who looked after spare horses which were needed to help the horse trams up certain hilly streets
tramp steamers, ships sailing on no regular route, but to wherever they had cargo to deliver
trio, a group of three people
turners, boys whose job was to unhitch tram horses at a terminus and lead them to be harnessed at the other end of the car
unanimously, with everyone in agreement
vaudeville, music hall variety show featuring individual acts
veterinary, concerning animal diseases
villa, large separate house in a city suburb
windjammer, word used to describe large sailing ships in the merchant navy.